Reality Mining

Reality Mining

Using Big Data to Engineer a Better World

Nathan Eagle and Kate Greene

The MIT Press
Cambridge, Massachusetts
London, England

© 2014 Massachusetts Institute of Technology

MIT Press books may be purchased at special quantity discounts for business or sales promotional use. For information, please email special_sales@mitpress.mit.edu.

This book was set in Stone Sans and Stone Serif by the MIT Press. Printed and bound in the United States of America.

Library of Congress Cataloging-in-Publication Data

Eagle, Nathan.
Reality mining : using big data to engineer a better world / Nathan Eagle and Kate Greene.
    p. cm
Includes bibliographical references and index.
ISBN 978-0-262-02768-7 (hardcover : alk. paper)
1. Data mining. 2. Big data. 3. Computer networks—Social aspects. 4. Information science—Social aspects. 5. Information science—Statistical methods. I. Greene, Kate, 1979– II. Title.
QA76.9.D343E24   2014
006.3′12—dc23
2013047165

10   9   8   7   6   5   4   3   2   1

Contents

Introduction

Big Data is all the rage. Conferences, books, research papers, and entrepreneurial interest on the topic abound. And with good reason: the idea of mining meaning from a previously unfathomable amount of data to identify clear trends and even to predict the future is certainly enchanting. But as all the conferences, books, research papers, and business plans illustrate, figuring out how to grapple with data on this scale and make good use of them is no simple task.

As we define it, Big Data is the collected bits of information produced from interactions that people and objects have with the digital, often networked world. The data can represent a single variable from an individual collected over years or multiple variables taken from hundreds of millions of people collected in an instant. Big Data can be long in time, voluminous in subject number (n), or broad in scope. Or it can be some combination of these three characteristics.

Thanks to the confluence of a variety of technological factors, Big Data is a fact of our modern world. Mobile, networked computers with powerful processors sit in your pocket, collecting data, crunching numbers, and sending bits to remote servers. Cloud computing and the ever-increasing density of

digital storage provides a home for all the information. Moreover, stream-processing paradigms allow data to be processed
over distributed machines. Availability of programming models
for large data sets, including MapReduce and the open-source
Hadoop, have made it possible to make sense of the torrents of
incoming information.

Big Data has been called the digital exhaust or the digital
footprints we leave in the wake of everyday activity; it is the
metadata of our lives. To some, the phrase evokes fear of a world
without privacy, of companies knowing more about us than we
know about ourselves, of governments keeping tabs on people
who the governments believe could pose a threat to their power.
To others, Big Data is a pot of gold at the end of a rainbow of
databases, an opportunity to capitalize on the next big information technology trend. And still others believe that some good
can actually be gleaned from the exabytes of data produced daily
by people all over the world.[1]

We, the authors of this book, are technologists who fall into
the latter category. We believe that if considered in a responsible, respectful, and context-aware way, Big Data can aid public
health, guide better individual decision making, foster the sharing of useful knowledge, and increase the rate of innovation.
The era of Big Data is here, and it isn't going to be over anytime
soon. It is important to ensure that individual liberties and free-
doms are maintained, that privacy isn't ignored, and that consumers are made aware of who accesses their data, when, and for
which purposes. We believe that within a conscientious context
of data collection, it's possible to use Big Data to engineer better
systems and potentially a better world. We use an approach we
call *Reality Mining*, which is not only about analyzing Big Data,
but about ensuring that the analysis reflects the reality of the

situation and the people involved, while being consistent with a conscientious data-collection approach.

The goal of this book, then, is to explore the positive potential of Big Data—specifically, to show how Reality Mining can be used to engineer better social systems. This means we introduce ideas meant to transcend simple, descriptive analytics such as bar graphs of pedometer data. We discuss ways to turn the data from observational maps of crimes or of disease outbreaks into meaningful actions or policies. We consider systems designed to use global, anonymous data. And we ask questions such as, "How can an early-warning system for disease epidemics be deployed in developing countries with limited public-health resources?" In essence, we want to explore how the use of Big Data can change people's lives for the better.

This book is divided into five parts. Each part addresses challenges and opportunities inherent to Big Data on various scales of data collection. Much in the same way that *Powers of Ten*, the 1977 short film by Charles Eames and Ray Eames, looks at the very small and very large parts of the universe, we address Big Data at small to increasingly larger scales.

We start our Reality-Mining journey at the individual scale, with data generated by and applied to a single person: the individual. From there, we move up a level to the neighborhood and organization, then to the city, followed by the nation, and finally the world. Admittedly, this framework is not absolute, nor is it applicable to all scenarios. Big Data collected at a particular scale can be applied at various other scales, of course. When appropriate, we mention some examples of this varied application. But as a way of thinking about the challenges inherent to collecting Big Data and making use of it, our five-level structure is a manageable one.

Each of the five parts in this book is divided into two chapters. The first chapter in each part details the type of data collected, the manner in which they are collected, and how, if possible, a reader might gain access to the data. The second chapter in each part details the applications and systems that have been built or we believe could be built based on the data.

Thus, the first chapter in each part serves as a guide to thinking about the various types of mineable data and how one might go about acquiring access to these data. Approaches to data acquisition range from creating a mobile app that collects sleep data to subscribing to a provider of air-traffic data to using the free and simple Google-based tools to parse search data. And in some cases, when data aren't easily accessible to most people, such as call data records from mobile phones, we offer suggestions for gaining limited access to the data or for finding emerging alternatives to the actual data.

Once you understand the type of data that can be mined, we discuss Reality-Mining applications that make use of it. Some of these systems exist, some are in early stages, and others haven't been explored at all. We provide information on just a handful of available applications and shine light on gaps where opportunities are available.

In writing this book, we considered addressing privacy issues in a separate chapter to display our consideration of the more troublesome issues with Big-Data collection and use. We ultimately decided against this approach. Engineers and businesses too often consider privacy of their users or customers after they have almost fully conceived their initial product. The privacy features then become add-ons, affixed after the main design is mostly complete. We did not want our book to mimic this approach. We believe that people's expectations of privacy and comfort level with sharing data should be considered from the beginning, baked deeply into any application or product design. Thus, throughout the book as needed, we reflect this sentiment by addressing issues of privacy, people's knowledge of how data are collected and shared, their comfort with these approaches (with comfort often a moving target affected by many variables), and privacy-conscious ways to build applications.

Importantly, this book leaves descriptions of specific analytic methodologies to other texts, academic papers, and discussions. The technical world of Big Data is sprawling. Practitioners of Reality Mining soon discover the multitudes of analytic techniques suitable for their data sets. Rather than proscribing particular analysis to data and applications (of which there are nearly infinite permutations), we choose to focus on the broader questions of Reality Mining: How do you engineer safe, respectful, and meaningful data collection? In what ways can you engineer practical and helpful human-centered systems?

So many conversations on Big Data seem to center around mining for "knowledge," as if "knowledge" were only as far as one can or should go. We propose a different view of Big Data, where we take a leap beyond descriptive analytics to actionable insights. Reality Mining is about using Big Data to develop systems that can affect positive change at all scales, from the individual to the global community. It is about using Big Data to build systems that improve our lives and make us healthier and that help us to live better, smarter, and happier among our 7 billion global neighbors.

I   The Individual (One Person)

1   Mobile Phones, Sensors, and Lifelogging: Collecting Data from Individuals While Considering Privacy

Never before has it been easier to collect so much daily data about ourselves. Technologies that track our habits, our location, our purchases, our routines, our social interactions, and our sentiments abound, from mobile phones and downloadable software to galvanic skin monitors and wearable cameras. Indeed, the ease with which the "data exhaust" is emitted and can be captured in the wake of our daily behaviors presents researchers with new opportunities not only to gain insight into those behaviors, but also to use these insights to better design systems to reflect how people actually behave.

Sensors, software, and their prevalence in our lives are important factors driving this trend. One significant set of sensors is embedded within today's mobile phone. With its rise in popularity and near necessity in daily life for people all over the world, the mobile phone is an undeniably essential tool for gathering data about the individual. By the end of 2012, there were nearly 6 billion mobile phone subscriptions currently worldwide.[1] And even the simplest phone leaves evidence of its owner's location with its service provider every time it pings a communication tower. Mobile phones, at first merely communication devices, have become constant computational companions that are increasingly being equipped with additional sensors. These accessories include accelerometers that are able to monitor our body movement, global positioning system (GPS) chipsets that measure our location, short-range radio protocols such as Bluetooth that can sense whom we are near, microphones that can infer what is happening around us, and even simple communication logs that are a measure of the evolution of our social networks.

A phone that is aware of a person's habits can make inferences about schedules, suggest activities, or provide reminders without any manual prompting. It can change its mode to accommodate various situations—for example, automatically turning off its ringer when in a movie theater and turning it back on after the film. A phone that knows more about your habits can recommend that you visit a bar where people with interests similar to yours gather or introduce you to a new restaurant just before you knew you wanted to try a new place for dinner.

Data from mobile phones can also provide insight into when and where people move from one location to another—information that can be critical when developing models of the spread of diseases such as malaria and flu. In addition, researchers are showing that changes in movement and conversation patterns captured by a phone with the appropriate sensors and software can indicate the onset of illnesses such as depression[2] or Parkinson's disease[3] earlier than other medical tests. These are just a few early-stage examples of the potential of Reality Mining, the idea of using personal data to make people's lives easier and healthier.

But it's not just mobile phones that keep track of us: a growing number of software applications monitor personal computer usage. Researchers hypothesize that the more a person knows about how long they spend on certain websites or reading and answering email, the more she can fine-tune her daily productivity. And, of course, as mobile phones become ever powerful computers, software that tracks the way people use phone applications has been built as well. Combining this watchful software with data from phone sensors and other applications, such as a calendar or contact list, is a powerful way to extrapolate behavioral information.

In addition to mobile phones and personal computers, people are increasingly signing up to wear specialized sensors throughout the day or during exercise or sleep, with the goal of providing insight into their physical habits and health. Google Glass is a head-mounted system that sports a small display, camera, microphone, processor, and wireless radio. It's gotten a great deal of attention as a way to stay constantly connected and to chronicle your life more easily by snapping pictures and recording video. More prosaically, unobtrusive pedometers and sleep monitors are gaining commercial traction. Data from these devices and applications on mobile phones that mimic many of these devices' functions can show a person precisely how physically active they are. Seeing such data can motivate people to live healthier lives. Another recent trend that has produced an enormous repository of personal data is the popularity of social-networking sites such as Facebook and Twitter, which allow people to post "status updates." With a short message, a user provides a snapshot into her life, answering questions such as "What are you doing?" "How do you feel?" "What's going on around you?" "What interests you right now?" Thus, status updates are akin, in some ways, to a user's answers to a sociologist's survey questions.

Once posted, these status updates are projected directly to people within a social network and, in some cases, to anyone who wants to look at these publicly available profiles online.

Some researchers are exploring ways to automate status updates based on information such as calendar events and location. Others are trying to make sense of these sentiments in aggregate; software developers have written simple programs to analyze the statements. Such programs often visualize the frequency of certain words used by increasing the font size for words that are used more often. In this way, people are able to see a snapshot of their activities and feelings over time.

A growing number of people have become fascinated with their personal data and combine all of the information about themselves they can acquire, be it from mobile phone communication, computer activity, biometric sensors, video recordings, or data recorded manually. This extreme sort of cataloging and quantifying is known as "lifelogging," and although it is not yet widespread, it has appealed to some people as a way to better understand all of their habits.

Lifelogging has gained traction mostly with engineers and designers who build web applications and other technology tools to make lifelogging easier. But as systems such as Google Glass and other lifelogging tools become available, and, importantly, as these tools become more integrated into people's daily lives, the activity of capturing moments will become less of a burden on the average person. It may even overcome the social stigma and be adopted by increasing numbers of less technologically savvy people.

In this chapter, we explore the ways in which an individual's data can be collected and logged, from a tacit, everyday interaction with a mobile phone to more purposeful digital announcements such as a status update. In addition, we discuss the privacy considerations that individuals, entrepreneurs, and big businesses need to keep in mind when collecting and analyzing the data as well as the privacy approaches currently in practice.

I   What Your Phone Knows

In the fall of 2004, 100 incoming and current MIT students were provided Nokia 6600 mobile phones that were loaded with a custom version of ContextPhones[4] that tracked cell tower IDs, application usage, and phone status such as whether the phone was idle or charging. Over the course of nine months, 300,000 hours of user data were logged for the MIT project.[5]

All participants were informed of the capabilities of the phones' logging software and were asked to sign a consent form[6] verifying that they understood what data their phones were collecting. Participants were able to erase the collected data at any time and turn off the logging function. As an additional privacy measure, the phone numbers of people outside the study were turned into a unique ID by a one-way (MD5) hash, making it impossible to retrieve the original number.

The Nokia 6600 was essentially a pack of sensors that the participants almost constantly wore. For years, researchers at universities and companies had been using sensors strategically placed in a room or office or sensor pack to collect data about a person's location, proximity to other people, and physical motion as well as even snippets of ambient sounds in that location.[7] Smart badges, with infrared or radio frequency identification (RFID) emitters and sensors designed to "see" other badges, had also been employed in projects to study workplace collaboration and social networking at conferences.[8] The sensors and smart badges were improvements from the days of wearing a backpack full of sensors and circuit boards, but still somewhat cumbersome.

Although there are as many different ways to affix sensors to people as there are computer science dissertations, the Nokia 6600 Reality-Mining project was unique in that it showed for the first time that researchers could track people's location, social interactions, and habits in a scalable way. At the time of the project, tens of millions of phones were capable of running the uberspyware loaded on the Nokia 6600s. This project proved that mobile phones could be a viable, scalable tool for ubiquitous computing and a way to gather more behavioral data than ever before. The information in the surveys that most sociologists use to learn about study participants' behaviors can't compare to the density and accuracy of data collected by the mobile phone.

Nokia 6600 phones were selected because they used the Symbian Series 60 software platform and could run a custom version of the Context software, developed at the University of Helsinki, which logged the individual phone's status: anything from making a call to charging to sitting idle. The phone came with 6 megabytes of internal memory and could accommodate a 32-megabyte MultiMediaCard flash memory card. The phones were unlocked and could be used with any local Global System for Mobile Communications mobile phone operator, including T-Mobile, AT&T, and Cingular (which since the time of the study has been acquired by AT&T). Custom applications could be added to the phone via the General Packet Radio Service data network, Bluetooth, memory card, or infrared port.

The phone continuously scanned and recorded Bluetooth devices within its vicinity. Bluetooth is a wireless protocol in the 2.4 to 2.48 gigahertz range, developed by Ericsson in 1994 and released in 1998 as a serial-cable replacement to connect different devices. Each Bluetooth-enabled device is capable of "device discovery," which allows the devices to seek out and find the Media Access Control address of other Bluetooth devices (BTID) within 5 to 10 meters.

The project used a modified version of the BlueAware application (MIDP2–Java for mobile devices) to record and time stamp the found BTIDs in a proximity log located on a server. However, using BlueAware to continually scan and log BTIDs depleted the phone battery within 18 hours, so the standard application was modified to scan the environment only once every five minutes, extending phone standby time to 36 hours. When dealing with mobile phones or other battery-powered devices, it's crucial to consider resource requirements of the sensors and consider workable alternatives to constant scanning.

A variation on BlueAware is called Bluedar, developed to work on a device that was fixed in locations where study participants gathered socially. Bluedar continuously scanned for visible devices and wirelessly transmitted detectable BTIDs to a server over an 802.11b wireless network. At the heart of the devices is a Bluetooth beacon that incorporates a class 2 Bluetooth chipset that can be controlled by an XPort web server, effectively able to detect any Bluetooth device within a range of 25 meters.

In addition to Bluetooth scans, the Nokia 6600 continuously logged cell tower IDs. There has been a significant amount of research that correlates cell tower ID with a user's location.[9] But obtaining accurate location information from cell towers is complicated by the fact that phones can detect cell towers that are several miles away, and in urban areas it's not uncommon to be within range of dozens of different towers.

For the study, relatively high location accuracy was achieved when a user spent enough time in one place to provide an estimate of the cell tower probability density function: phones in the same location can be connected to different cell towers at different times depending on a variety of variables, including signal strength and network traffic. Thus, over time, each phone "sees" a number of different cell towers, and the distribution of detected towers can vary substantially with even small changes in location. Cell tower ID can also be cross-referenced with static Bluetooth devices, such as a desktop computer, to narrow down a location.

Of course, today a mobile phone can log its user's location in a number of other, straightforward ways. Many smart phones are equipped with GPS chips, and companies such as Google and Skyhook use a combination of location-triangulation means to eke out a phone's location from Wi-Fi base-station signals, cell towers, and GPS (which is less accurate when used indoors). However, for simple phones, using a cell tower ID is still the cheapest, easiest, and least obtrusive way to log location.

In the early part of the MIT Nokia 6600 experiment, the data collected were stored on the phone's limited internal memory, making it necessary to frequently dump the data to the researchers. The process took about five minutes and allowed the researchers to install upgrades to the application. However, as one month of data amounted to approximately 5 to 10 megabytes, it made sense to store some of it on the phone's removable flash memory card. With modifications to the program to write more efficiently to the flashcard, data collection was eventually postponed for months. In addition, some participants later used T-Mobile's limited Internet service to email the data to a proxy server.

Finally, study participants completed surveys asking them about their mobile phone usage, their daily behavior patterns, their satisfaction with MIT, their social circle, and their work group. In addition, the last question included a list of every study participant and asked the subject to rate his or her frequency of interaction with any of the others on the list and whether any of them was in the subject's circle of friends. These surveys complemented the primary data sets from the phone and helped to put analysis of the data in perspective.

The findings of the 100-person study were encouraging. With the use of computational tools called "eigenbehaviors," the results indicated that a person's location, proximity to other people, call logs, and phone activity at the beginning of the day often indicate only a small possibility of behaviors later in the evening.[10] For instance, if a person woke up at 10:00 a.m. on a Saturday, it was possible to predict, with surprisingly high accuracy, that he would be with certain people at a certain place later in the evening. In addition, analysis of communication and proximity data revealed relationships and positions within social networks such as whether a subject was an MIT freshman, a graduate student, or a professor. Potential applications that can make use of these results are discussed in the next chapter.

Since the time of this study, projects that use mobile phone sensors have cropped up at universities and in company labs, and there are a number of variations on the data-collection themes outlined by the MIT/Nokia project in 2003. For example, in a 2009 project called SoundSense, from Hong Lu and other researchers at Dartmouth University, software was loaded onto an iPhone to capture ambient sound to give contextual awareness in an energy-efficient and privacy-sensitive way.[11] The hypothesis was that a phone can know when a person is in an important meeting from certain audio cues and might direct calls from certain people directly to voicemail while letting others through.

One notable example and publicly accessible way to track phone activity is called Funf, an open-sensing framework spun out of MIT's Media Lab. The Funf framework allows data collection from various "probes" on the phone: GPS, location, accelerometer, call log, running apps, screen state, and battery status, for example, all stored and encrypted locally on the phone. Whereas Funf is a framework that allows any programmer to build software to suit his or her needs, Funf Journal is a ready-made app for Android phones that stores data from various probes on the phone in an encrypted state, which is key to protecting user data. It also provides a way for people to download their data to a computer or upload those data to a remote server for analysis.[12]

In addition to Funf, numerous commercial spyware applications are available for both the phone and personal computers that can be an important part of the data-collection toolkit for someone who might not have the means to develop his or her own personal software. In particular, software for monitoring productivity on computers—how much time is spent on certain websites and using certain applications—has become a cottage industry in itself.

II Software That Watches Your Habits

The MIT Reality-Mining project provides a specific example of setting up a mobile phone–based study to collect personal data. One of the tools used in the project was specialized software from the University of Helsinki that tracked the state of the phone: when it was in use for a call, when it was charging, when it was turned off, for example. Although this software may not be available to the average person, other software options can provide a log of the way a phone is used. And in some cases, software can log GPS data, obviating the need to go through a mobile operator or triangulating a Wi-Fi signal to get location data.

A quick web search turns up a number of sites that sell software to be installed on iPhones, BlackBerrys, Android phones, and Windows Mobile and Symbian operating system phones.[13] The software is targeted at parents worried about their teens' phone activity and whereabouts, at employers who want to monitor employees' use of company-supplied phones, and at people who want to catch spouses they suspect of cheating. It's important to note that different regions have different laws for collecting data from people's mobile phones, and to do so legally, permission from the person who owns the phone or ownership of the device and/or contract is required.[14]

The tracking software is loaded onto the phone and runs in the background, logging activity by those on the phone. These logs are then sent to a server and are accessible through a website. Call logs can be collected, including incoming and outgoing number, duration, and time stamp. Entire text messages can be stored on remote servers even after the phone's logs are deleted. GPS location can be logged when a signal is available. Depending on the phone, website uniform resource locators (URLs) can be recorded as well.

Comparable commercial spyware for personal computers is also available. Such spyware is marketed mostly to people who are interested in self-monitoring their computer activities to help them increase their own productivity. Throughout the world, millions of people spend their work hours using computers and applications such as email, chats, web browsers (and web pages), as well as word-, image-, and video-processing software—essentially any software that runs on a computer. Software applications such as Slife, RescueTime, Klok, SlimTimer, and WorkTime from Nestersoft Inc., to name a few, are designed to track the time spent running different applications in the foreground of the system and then to provide feedback to the user.

The software can be installed on a computer or run from a website. In some cases, a person can share information collected from these watchful services by tagging certain activities, such as reading news stories, as "public" information. She can also set goals for the amount of time spent in certain applications—for instance, 30 minutes answering emails in the morning. She can see progress toward her goals in visualization and can set up reminders to change tasks if she's spent too long using one application.

In addition to automatically logging information about the person using a device, there is a growing trend toward survey-based software specifically for mobile phones. In the fall of 2009, the company Techneos launched SODA, a system that lets people, researchers, and companies create surveys for mobile phones. Because mobile phones are, for many people, always nearby, a mobile phone survey, unlike an online survey, can target a person at a specific time of day or at a specific location, and it can be less obtrusive than a phone call.

SODA can be an interesting tool for people looking to collect data for Reality Mining because people can provide much more information than usually available in simple answers to survey questions. Location data can be included if the participants agree to it, and participants can also include pictures that are relevant to questions. The platform is flexible in terms of the type of questions that can be asked—multiple choice, sliding scale, open numeric, open text, audio file, image file, and even barcode input. In addition, it can be targeted to a range of languages, including Chinese, English, French, Portuguese, Spanish, German, Hindi, Japanese, and Thai.[15]

III   Biosensors on the Body

Productivity, communication logs, and surveys, as recorded by a computer or a phone, supply only part of the picture of a person's day and life, however. Biometric sensors can fill in the gaps, giving precise information about physiological changes that occur during various times of day and during various activities. To get this information, researchers and individuals—often those with chronic illnesses—have turned to specialized hardware systems that track pulse, blood pressure, skin conductivity, and other metrics and in some cases that allow them to manually record symptoms, diet, and exercise.

BodyMedia is a large, established company that offers devices and a web service for tracking activity and providing reminders about health goals. CardioNet offers a portable electrocardiogram (ECG) system. Products such as the FitBit pedometer, the Nike+ exercise-tracking system, Polar and Garmin GPS watches, and the Withing's Wi-Fi-connected scale have also gained traction in the marketplace. (The Zeo Personal Sleep Coach also found market success as a sleep tracker using a wireless headband that transmitted data to a bedside alarm clock or a mobile phone, but unfortunately the company dissolved in early 2013.) In addition, mobile phone applications that make use of the gadget's accelerometers and GPS sensors, for instance, are also starting to play a growing role in collecting biometric information. Table 1.1 is a list of some commercial technologies that log biological data.

Software developers have also made phone applications that can provide some of the same functionality of dedicated sleep trackers, albeit with variable accuracy. iSleepTracker and Sleep Cycle are examples of apps that use the iPhone's accelerometers

Table 1.1
Various Commercially Available Sensor Products: Purpose, Features, and Interfaces

Product	Purpose	Features	Interface
Body Media FIT by Body Media	Tracks sleep quality and calories expended and consumed, mainly for weight-loss purposes.	Armband that contains a three-axis accelerometer that tracks motion, a thermometer that measures skin temperature, a galvanic skin-response sensor that tracks water content, and a heat flux sensor that measures heat dissipated from the body.	Simple LED indicator on armband; more detailed data are available on the website, to which users regularly upload data from the device.
Mobile Cardiac Outpatient Telemetry by CardioNet	Tracks heartbeats for irregularities and other problems.	A small, wearable ECG system that tracks all heartbeats 24 hours a day for up to 21 days.	Electrical leads attached to a person's chest transmit electrical signals to a small portable monitor worn around a patient's neck. When an abnormality occurs, the monitor wirelessly sends data to a center, where they are further analyzed and reported to doctors.
FitBit Tracker by FitBit, Inc.	Tracks certain types of low-impact physical activity and sleep quality.	A small, unobtrusive pedometer clips to pants or a bra (and in a wristband at night). It lasts 10 days before it needs to be recharged.	An in-home base station wirelessly transmits data from the pedometer to the company's server, where it is uploaded to a website that summarizes the data.

Table 1.1 (cont.)

Product	Purpose	Features	Interface
Zeo Personal Sleep Coach by Zeo, Inc. (company dissolved in 2013)	Tracks brain and face muscle activity during sleep.	Consists of a headband that measures electrical activity that corresponds to sleep stage and quality. The data are wirelessly sent to a specialized alarm clock that gently awakes a person in his or her lightest stage of sleep.	A specialized alarm clock displays sleep information and a web service that analyzes it and tries to correlate sleep quality to various lifestyle factors.
iSleepTracker by Innovative Sleep Solutions	Tracks sleep activity and quality.	A wristwatchlike device tracks sleep activity.	A website provides analysis and visualization.
HRS-I by WIN Human Recorder	Tracks heartbeats for irregularities and other problems as well as body temperature and movements.	A small sensor pack that attaches to a person's chest that can last for three to four days on a charge.	Data are transmitted to a mobile phone or computer and can be viewed online.
Garmin Forerunner 910XT GPS device	Records time, distance, elevation, and heart rate on land and swim distance, efficiency, stroke count, and pool lengths in water.	A wristwatchlike device that tracks various modes of physical exertion and geographic movement.	Wirelessly transfers data to Garmin Connect, an online site for analysis and sharing.

to measure movement on a bed. Similarly, Smart Alarm, an Android application, estimates a sleeper's sleep stage. Because these applications indirectly measure a person's movement (and results vary based on number of people and animals in the bed as well as firmness of mattress), the main purpose seems to be to wake up a sleeper when she is in the lightest sleep stage, staving off grogginess that can come from waking up during deep sleep.

Nike+ makes use of devices such as iPhones, Android phones, and iPods that people already use to listen to music while running. It tracks steps using a pedometer that can be clipped onto shoes or inserted in specialized Nike footwear, and wirelessly transmits the data to the phone or music player. When the gadgets are synced to the Internet for updates via a user's computer, the Nike+ data are uploaded to Nike's site, where a user can see his or her progress and virtually compete with other runners. The system is focused mainly on helping people who are actively running or walking to keep track of their workouts.

Similarly, RunKeeper, Runtastic, and Runmeter are mobile phone applications that use GPS to track people's outdoor activity where GPS signal strength is contingent upon direct line-of-site to GPS satellites. A person may manually enter activities that aren't outdoors, such as swimming at a pool, and allow their iPhone to sync with gym equipment, such as a treadmill, that provides workout outputs. As with all of the other systems, an online dashboard is used to see progress and keep track of goals.

RunKeeper has collaborated with Withings, a company that makes Wi-Fi-enabled scales so that when a person weighs herself on a Withings scale, the data is automatically logged on RunKeeper's site. This information is used when RunKeeper roughly calculates the number of calories burned based on the speed with which a person travels over a certain distance.

Each of these apps and devices provides various levels of user control over the way the data it collected are exported by the user. In some cases, in-app analysis is provided for free or with a fee for more advanced options. In the case of Body Media, a researcher must purchase a special license for access to all the data the armband collects. In order for individual Body Media customers who are not participating in a research study to access the data the armband collects, they must purchase a subscription to the company's online services and provide a significant amount of personal information to use the analysis tools. Although these products are providing more insights into the body than ever before, customers should read the fine print in product agreements to know exactly how the data are collected and used and whether the company or the customer retains ownership of it. Chapter 2 discusses more concerns over data ownership.

IV   What Are You Doing?

Many biometric sensors and mobile phone applications are capable of sending out a message to a third party, be it a doctor or a public website where fitness data are publicly available. In essence, people are providing "status updates" about their physical condition. But status updates of all sorts have lately gained traction with the general public, providing a wealth of information about people's habits and activities.

A number of activity-tracking apps can now automatically update Twitter or Facebook statuses when an activity such as running or biking is complete. The Dartmouth project Sound-Sense, mentioned previously, uses the microphone of a mobile phone to infer a person's location and activity, information that could be used to provide simple status updates, such as whether a person is in a coffee shop, walking outside, or brushing his or her teeth, for example. The software captures bits of sound and, using machine learning techniques, guesses general sounds such as music or a human voice and discovers new sounds unique to a user, while keeping privacy in mind. In all cases, the raw audio is preprocessed so that features are extracted. The original audio is not saved, and the features alone don't provide enough information to re-create it.

V   Lifelogging: Capturing the Flow of Data

Clearly, there are myriad ways to collect data about the individual. It's also clear that there currently is no unified method for collecting different types of data, which may be captured automatically, inferred by software, or produced and logged manually. But a growing subset of people are trying to create such a method for logging part or all of their lives: anything about themselves that can be quantified.

Lifelogging as a trend is somewhat more popular in communities of technically oriented people. Some of these people have created Internet and mobile phone applications for logging data, specialized hardware such as wearable cameras for capturing video and images, and spreadsheet templates for recording a range of daily behaviors such as types of food consumed and emotions felt. Lifelogging fills in the gaps left by other data-collection methods and attempts to combine all the data in a cohesive framework that explains the individual quantitatively.

Ultimately, this type of work has a boundless potential. One obvious application is that lifelogging allows people to see their habits and how small changes in behaviors affect the rest of their lives, but there are more far-reaching possibilities as well. Today, no one really knows what the longitudinal indicators of, say, a heart attack are. But with more people self-surveilling so many aspects of their lives—and making it public, as is the trend—it might be possible for researchers to look back over a person's months or years of data and determine correlations, possible causes, and potential indicators of a severe medical event.

Some of the most compelling lifelogging projects involve automatically capturing images and video. In late 2009, Vicon, a company that makes motion-capture systems, licensed technology developed at Microsoft to manufacture and sell a wearable camera that automatically takes a series of pictures throughout the day.[16] Microsoft's SenseCam hardware consists of a wide-angle lens and a number of different electronic sensors, including light-intensity and light-color sensors, a passive infrared (body heat) detector, a temperature sensor, and a multiple-axis accelerometer. SenseCam can be programmed to take a picture at a regular interval or when changes in the wearer or environment, recorded by the sensors, trigger a photograph to be taken.[17]

Today, Google is promoting its lifelogging device, Glass, which sports a heads-up display, camera, microphone, processor, and wireless functions—all inside the frame of a pair of lens-free glasses.[18] With a voice prompt, the camera can take pictures or video. Because the display is networked, it can show text messages and provide navigational directions. Google allows programmers to build their own apps for the device, from games to news alerts. It's still early days for this product, which has received quite a bit of hype. No one knows how popular it will eventually be outside tech circles, but it's likely just the first iteration of this sort of wearable technology.

Other small, wearable cameras are the GoPro and Contour wearable video cameras, designed for extreme athletes. Both come with a number of different types of mounts so the cameras can be affixed to a helmet or worn on a chest harness, for instance. Another wearable video camera, called Loocxie, is small and light enough that it can be mounted around the ear.

A number of online blogs aggregate information about various lifelogging devices, systems, and software, some of them mentioned earlier in this chapter. *Total Recall* by Gordon Bell and Jim Gemmell and *The Quantified Self* by Kevin Kelly are popular blogs that cover lifelogging. Gordon Bell of Microsoft is known as one of the most prolific lifeloggers and has been collecting personal data for years in a project called MyLifeBits.[19] The project is accessible online, where pictures, videos, phone call recordings, personal letters, and greeting cards are sorted and searchable.

To log your life, it's helpful to begin with a guide,[20] and people sometimes start by focusing on one aspect of their lives—such as when they go to sleep and wake up—and expand to other areas where recording data isn't as daunting. One system that focuses on a single metric is called Track Your Happiness.[21] It's a project out of Harvard in which automated text messages are sent to a participant's mobile phone. The messages contain a link that opens a short survey about what the person is doing and how they feel about it. After weeks of answering questions multiple times a day, a person is provided a "happiness report" that visualizes the participant's responses.

Another system, called your.flowing.data,[22] allows people to send to an online database a direct message via Twitter about what they are doing. For the most accurate log, it helps to follow a proscribed template in the messages, such as "reading X" or "watching X." The your.flowing.data system automatically logs the time the message is sent, thereby providing a time stamp, and the site provides visualization of the frequency of activities.

DailyDiary[23] is a site that sends out email prompts asking people specific, preselected questions such as "How was your day?" and "What did you eat today?" Members of the site answer questions, get ratings, and are able to participate in an online community, seeing how others are progressing toward goals.

Although these tools allow people to log and organize more information about their lives in a digital way, they lack a crucial characteristic: they are not easy to use and to remember to use. As long as lifelogging relies heavily on manual data entry, with an objective to collect as much as possible, it will remain a fringe activity because most people only selectively and sparsely record their life events.

VI Conclusion

A person can self-track parts of his or her life and habits in a growing number of ways, and there is more and more software that does much of this tracking passively, behind the scenes, without input from a person using the tracking software. Some people would argue that personalized data collection won't take off until it can happen without a person constantly tending to a device, entering data, and fiddling with settings. Others believe that people should always be in the loop of personal data collection so they can choose exactly what they want saved and how and where they want it stored.

It's likely that a combination of the two approaches will persist in personal-data-collection techniques for a while. Each person has his or her own tolerance for making information about himself or herself publicly available, so the best approach that self-tracking services can take is to offer a range of privacy settings that are easily readable and understandable by their customers. And still others will be more than happy to offload the task of data collection to specific devices, checking in only when they want to look back at an event or idea that was automatically logged.

Now, more than ever, software developers need to be sensitive to human psychology and sociology. They need to understand the factors that motivate a person to log specific events or activities in their lives and those that make it a daily habit. They need to understand how to present passively logged data to a person in a way that doesn't seem creepy or intrusive. They need to learn how to make those devices that track the data of our lives helpful and not burdensome. And in the case of lifelogging devices, they need to be aware that even the presence of such technology can dramatically alter social dynamics. We're still finding out how people respond with the knowledge that anyone wearing Google Glass, friend or stranger, can record anything they do or say, unobtrusively and without their permission. The next chapter explores specific applications of data at the individual scale while addressing some of the sensitivity concerns mentioned in this chapter.

2 Using Personal Data in a Privacy-Sensitive Way to Make a Person's Life Easier and Healthier

Once a person's various streams of data exhaust are collected, the question still remains: What can be done with them? This chapter provides a variety of answers to that question, including descriptions of specific projects with goals to make systems that help people lead healthier and more enjoyable lives. The projects discussed in this chapter are generally still in their early stages and just scratching the surface of data mining at the individual level.

One exciting application is to use an individual's data analysis to develop services that act as a personal coach, giving prompts to help a person change his behaviors. The coach could, for instance, gently remind a person to talk more or less during company meetings, to curb hours spent surfing certain websites, and even to quit smoking. Devices on the market, such as pedometers and calorimeters, already provide feedback about health-related habits in an attempt to get people to be more physically active and conscious of what they eat. Taking it a step further to prompt a person toward a specific action could make the difference in whether she actually achieves her goals.

Personal data analysis can also be built into systems that notify people when something happens that's out of the ordinary, potentially dangerous to someone, or indicative of property damage or theft. Systems can be built that track a person's location for safety purposes or to determine if a car has been stolen.

This chapter doesn't come close to providing an exhaustive list of all possible projects that use data at this level. Rather, it's an exploration of a number of areas in which researchers and entrepreneurs are already or might start thinking of their own projects. Many applications of individual data are cropping up every day—some of them will persist, others will be short-lived, but they increasingly point toward a trend in making use of data to benefit the people who create those data.

Regardless of the application, it's clear that the implications of projects and products built from mined personal data instantly raise important questions of personal privacy. Who and what entities have access to someone's personal data? Do data belong to the people who create them, or do they belong to the people who own the technology that captures and curates them? There's currently no standard.

Can auto insurance companies use information on the places that a person drives to in order to charge a higher premium? Health insurance companies already provide discounts to people who wear pedometers, proving that they are active and, presumably, less expensive health-care consumers. Might health insurance companies track more than steps? How about a person's smoking habits or their social network? Credit card companies already charge higher interest rates to people who shop at certain stores due to the debt profiles of other people who shop at those stores. Is it fair that companies who have access to data should receive a greater benefit than the individual who provides the data?

These questions are still open, but in this chapter we explore some of the privacy and policy ramifications of collecting personal data and trends that indicate the ways in which these ramifications might be managed in the future. In addition, we investigate what can be done to ensure that people have as much control as possible over who sees and uses their personal data exhaust.

I   Breaking Bad Habits

When a person has a bad habit, she may have a vague or only a partial concept of the sort of environmental stimuli that trigger the habit. If she had quantitative data that link behaviors, locations, and social situations to the habit, however, she might be able to change her ways.

A clever example of using personal data to improve a person's health, still in the early stages, seeks to find which behaviors, locations, and social interactions are associated with smoking. If the factors that contribute to someone lighting up are known, engineers can feasibly build a mobile phone application, for instance, that recognizes a potential smoking situation. It might provide feedback, such as prompting the smoker to chew a piece of gum instead. It's also reasonable to assume that the methods developed in the smoking research project might be applied to other types of behavior such as general substance abuse, high-risk sexual activity, nutrition, and exercise.

In particular, this project, proposed by Nathan Eagle and his colleagues,[1] aims to study young-adult smokers ages 18 to 25. These smokers sometimes smoke as little as a cigarette a month, but recent research has suggested that even at such low levels tobacco can be addictive over time.[2] Young adults are particularly interesting to study because the rate at which they smoke surpasses all other age groups—up to 38 percent.[3]

It's estimated that half the occasional smokers continue smoking after four years of college, but the other half quit after this time.[4] This indicates a transition time for those who occasionally smoke in college; it's a crucial time in which occasional smokers can be steered toward quitting—and this is where the mobile phone comes in.

The idea of using a mobile phone to help someone stop smoking isn't novel. In fact, already-existing antismoking campaigns use the Internet and mobile devices to send tobacco education and treatment to youth and young adults.[5] However, the proposed project by Eagle and his colleagues, called Ecological Momentary Assessment, aims to use mobile phones to collect real-time data to measure the impact of peer relationships and interactions on an individual's smoking habits and ability to quit. The project combines elements from the original MIT Reality-Mining project (see chapter 1), in which spyware is loaded onto mobile phones with simple surveys that allow people to answer questions about their behavior as it happens.

Mobile phones, with their collection of sensors and prevalence among young adults, make a good fit for a project to study smoking behavior. The project proposes to collect 100 City University of New York students who smoke at least one cigarette per month. They all will be provided with a software utility that automatically detects and uploads behavioral data, including movement via GPS, communication via phone logs, and proximity to other people via Bluetooth.

In addition to these sensors, the study participants will also answer questions via their mobile devices that capture smoking behavior, social and environmental contexts conducive to smoking, urges to smoke, and strategies to cope with these urges. Because the phone logs contain information about a person's social network at the time of these surveys, they provide an eco-logically valid representation of the people and the setting that affect the subjects' smoking. This information can then be used to inform the smoker of effective social supports to help him or her stop smoking.

The ultimate goal of the project is to create predictors that cat-egorize the aspects of a smoker's life that contribute to his smok-ing habit more accurately than a human observer could. The first step to do this is to build algorithms that can recognize the structure of a person's daily, weekly, and monthly routine. The idea of mapping a person's actions in a way that reveals routine and predictability has been shown in various earlier projects,[6] but when mobile phones are used to determine this structure, they provide more accuracy than any other method used today.

The study has far-reaching implications. From a practical standpoint, it could be used in clinical care to answer ques-tions about social networks that were previously invisible using observational data alone. In the future, clinicians could identify members of social networks who could be the most beneficial to help a person stop smoking. In addition, the information from the study could be used to improve the current mobile phone intervention methods, including the possibility of an applica-tion that could recognize possible scenarios in which a person is inclined to smoke and could prompt her to resist temptation.

On the theoretical research front, the project could shed light on complex interactions between social, environmental, and psychological determinants that researchers have for years sus-pected affect young adult smoking habits. For instance, there is some debate around whether young adult smokers volun-tarily associate with other people who smoke or if they and their

friends pick up the habit within the same time frame. Differen-
tiating these two cases could be crucial for designing effective
interventions.

And finally, the methods used in the mobile phone study
could be broadly applied to studies about habits other than
smoking. In fact, other researchers are exploring similar methods
to address different behavioral issues. In one study at Accenture,
engineers have developed a project that effectively monitors the
length of time that people in a meeting or in conversations are
talking.[7] The system uses the microphone on a person's mobile
phone and stores data about the conversations on a central
server. The goal is for people to become more aware of their conversation dynamics, something that's often difficult to self-mon-
itor. Importantly, however, the system has integrated prompts,
sent to the phone, when a person has exceeded a certain threshold of talk time or has remained silent for a certain length of
time, depending on the situation. The real-time analysis and
feedback could help people navigate social or business situations
more effectively.

In a similar vein, behavior-monitoring software on computers could be used to change bad habits. Software discussed in
chapter 1, such as Slife, RescueTime, Klok, SlimTimer, and Work-
Time, tracks the time spent in different applications on a computer and provides feedback to the user. Some of these programs
allow people to visualize their computer habits and specify goals
about how and when they use certain applications. Although
some of these programs have the ability to analyze the behavior in a way that could be used to develop strategies for changing habits, more could be done with the data. Instead of simple
timed prompts, groups of employees, for instance, could play
social games that have them directly compete with each other in

the completion of certain tasks. Productivity-monitoring tools are a prime example of a field that's ready for engineers to build innovative tools to further improve productivity.

II Out of the Ordinary

Another way to use personal data is to build a monitoring system that indicates when someone's behavior extends significantly outside the norm into possibly harmful or dangerous territory. The idea of watching behaviors closely and alerting someone about something abnormal naturally raises the hackles of most people who prize their privacy; however, if used ethically, such systems could be useful in a number of scenarios, such as getting earlier notification of a stolen car and alerting a caretaker that his patient is acting in an unsafe way.

The key to such a system is collecting a range of data about a person's whereabouts and social interactions and analyzing it to determine a person's eigenbehaviors or the scope of an individual's normal behaviors, as discussed in chapter 1.

In the instance of elder-care monitoring, eigenbehaviors can be used to detect when an event occurs that is far outside of a user's so-called behavior space. A person's behavior space is essentially a mathematical representation of his behaviors that consists of a number of different variables that are dependent upon one another. An event outside a person's behavior space isn't simply something that a person hasn't done before. Based on analysis, it is something that is so improbable considering any other prior behaviors that it has a high likelihood of being unintended or potentially dangerous.

For example, imagine an elderly person who gets on a bus at 11:00 p.m. and takes it to a part of his city where he has rarely been before and in which none of his known social contacts live or frequent. A mobile phone or other wearable device that has kept track of this person's movement and is aware of his social contacts and calendar could determine if this behavior is far outside his normal scope of behaviors. Depending on the settings of such a monitoring system, the elderly person himself could be notified and asked to respond to a prompt, or a caregiver could be alerted.

Several companies, such as General Electric as well as smaller start-ups, are racing to establish their niche in the rapidly expanding market for monitoring the elderly.[8] In many cases, the systems use a number of distributed sensors around a person's house. Although the sensors are able to determine certain behaviors, such as preparing meals, with high accuracy, their installation and maintenance, which can be difficult and expensive, might be limiting factors for some companies and for the field in general.

An eigenbehavior-based system like this could also be implemented in antitheft systems in cars. Although there already are a number of radio-enabled car-locating systems, including LoJack and GM's OnStar, that can identify where a car is after it's been stolen, an eigenbehavior-based system can be more proactive. Such a system could determine if a car is being driven at an unusual time of day to an unusual area, and then it could check in with the owners to make sure that they're aware of their car's whereabouts.

III Big Personal Data and Big Privacy Considerations

All Reality-Mining applications work perfectly in a theoretical world, of course. Reality-Mining research projects run smoothly because subjects understand the terms of the project, and they trust that the researchers are scrupulous and will protect the integrity and privacy of their data. They also know that the research project will eventually end; they have opted to have their data analyzed, and they can opt out without repercussion or major loss of benefit.

The transition from research project to real-world application is tricky, however. How exactly can privacy be safeguarded if a third-party company is collecting the data and providing feedback? Interestingly, the individual level of data collection may in fact be the most manageable in terms of privacy, thanks to some fundamental characteristics of mobile phones. There are plenty of options for gathering and storing data in the cloud or on a company's remote server, but they aren't the only places to do so. Mobile phones have the capability to store data locally, on the device itself. Because processing power and solid-state storage capacity effectively double in mobile phones every two years, thus giving a tiny handheld device computing capabilities of a much larger machine just a few years earlier, Reality-Mining tasks can be contained on the phone. Increased computing and storage of phones means data need not necessarily be uploaded to a remote server for processing or storage or shared with a third party. That said, the vast majority of data analysts are taking a hybrid approach that uses a combination of local mobile phone software and software on a remote server. However, because of the Electronic Communications Privacy Act of 1986, it is possible in some cases that when a person's data are on the server, law enforcement and government officials can search those data with only a subpoena and without a warrant. Data stored on a personal computing device, however, still require a warrant to be searched.[9]

Even so, the vast majority of companies that provide personal data-collection options to consumers opt for the hybrid approach. The data that are collected and stored on remote servers can often be analyzed to improve the product. In other cases, the data themselves are of high value to the company because its intention is to target its customers with its advertisements. So although there's a technological opportunity for consumers to have more control over their data exhaust, in practice they may realistically not have the options to do so. In addition, it takes a fair amount of technical savvy to realize the difference between data storage or processing that happens on the software of your phone and on a remote server, especially on smart phones, where applications are often interacting with the network in the background. And it takes a significant mental load to keep track of the terms of service of all of the scattered applications that people use: Which ones share data with other companies? Which ones allow your data to expire? Have the terms of service been updated? How broadly? Can you move your data to another application if you're not happy with the services you're being provided?

Nevertheless, if there's ever a realm to establish solid terms of data ownership, it's at the individual level. Therefore, new rules for data ownership and privacy need to be written by companies, consumers, activist groups, and lawmakers. After all, it doesn't take much imagination to come up with uses of personal data and analysis that are used to control, intimidate, or extort people. Could a health insurance company increase a person's premium if it finds out that he is hanging out with friends that make him more likely to smoke and less likely to exercise? Who does the technology benefit if an abusive caretaker is informed that an elderly person is en route to a safer location? Can police track your whereabouts if you're accused of stalking or domestic abuse? Can car insurance companies have access to data on a person's most frequently used routes and charge them accordingly?

In the past couple of years, all of these issues have appeared in headlines as local governments are dealing with the implications of the abundance of personal and public sensors. Some of these questions are starting to get answered. The following sections briefly lay out three important applications in which it will become increasingly important to consider a new type of data privacy and ownership: health-wellness incentives, pay-as-you-drive auto insurance, and prevention of domestic violence and caretaker abuse. Although these three topics only begin to touch on the possible complications that come with thinking about individual data collection, they are a start and could lead to solutions that might be more broadly applied to different areas.

IV   Health Self-Surveillance for Insurance Savings

The idea of financially penalizing a person for unhealthy habits isn't common, and today the approach that's most often used is a so-called health-incentive program, in which participants are rewarded money for choosing healthier habits instead of being penalized for unhealthy ones. In fact, the past few years have seen an increase in the number of companies in the "health-incentive management" industry. These companies help employers provide incentives for employees who participate in wellness programs and actively change their lifestyles to become healthier.

Companies working in this industry—such as Virgin Health-Miles, RedBrick Health, and Tangerine Wellness, to name a few—work directly with employers to try to mitigate the number of health insurance claims made by employees in order ultimately to save employers money. With their extra money, employers then decide how to incentivize their employees. Some reduce deductibles; others decrease premiums or copayments.

There are generally two types of programs. One type financially rewards participants for participating in a health-related class, such as a smoking-cessation program, and the other type financially rewards a person if he meets a specific health target, such as reducing his weight by 30 pounds by a certain date.[10] In both instances, it's possible to reduce one's health-care premium by $100 or more each month.

Sensors such as pedometers, phone-based accelerometers, heart-rate monitors, and online data-logging sites are playing an increasingly important role in such wellness programs. Some programs use pedometers, for instance, to hold "challenges" that employees participate in. Others use these monitors to help people set health-target goals. If a person doesn't do well in the program, then there are no financial penalties, just a lost opportunity to save. The programs are voluntary, but they are becoming popular. Participation rates are 80 percent for some companies.[11]

Making such programs voluntary and framing the monetary exchange as "savings" as opposed to "penalties" is likely an important semantic distinction that has helped the programs gain participation in the past few years. In 2007 and 2008, companies including Black & Decker and Whirlpool began experimenting with fines for employees who smoked. And in 2008, Whirlpool suspended employees who lied to avoid a $500 annual tobacco surcharge. However, this action prompted at least one company, the Tribune Co., to drop a smoker penalty, indicating that some companies might be opting for the carrot rather than the stick.[12]

Although wellness programs have been around for decades, their numbers and the sophistication of the technology they use will likely grow. Sensors are getting less expensive and coming in smaller packages, and, importantly, some legislative actions are pushing the industry forward. In the spring of 2010, US president Barack Obama signed a bill that outlines provisions to increase the number of businesses that offer wellness programs, increase the number of employees who participate, more effectively track programs, and improve overall program effectiveness.[13] Without doubt, the programs make financial sense to most companies that use them. The Wellness Council of America claims that a $1 investment in a program translates into $3 worth of health-care savings.[14]

But what about employee privacy? According to a 2008 amendment to the Americans with Disabilities Act (ADA), employers can't ask an employee about medical conditions unless the query is "job related and consistent with business necessity."[15] However, according to a 2002 Equal Employment Opportunity Commission (EEOC) enforcement guide, employers may conduct voluntary medical histories that are part of an employee health program even if the questions aren't job related or consistent with business necessity. And the Health Insurance Portability and Accountability Act (HIPAA) of 1996 and subsequent legislation in 2006 allow employer plans to vary premiums, deductibles, and copayments as part of an employee wellness program. Nondiscrimination provisions within HIPAA prohibit charging individuals with similar health status different amounts. But it's unclear how some aspects of HIPAA and newer regulations can be reconciled with the EEOC's requirement that programs be voluntary and in line with the ADA's privacy provisions.[16]

An additional challenge is one of fundamental fairness. One of the most important conditions of these early bills is that the reward must not exceed 20 percent of the cost of the individual employee's coverage. However, the bill signed by Obama in 2010 increases that amount to 30 percent, a rate that some organizations believe could put a disproportionate burden on low-wage workers who are generally less likely to be as healthy as high-wage workers.[17]

These questions are going to be front and center as more employers implement wellness programs in an attempt to reign in the increasing costs of health-care insurance. And with more accurate sensors and algorithms that determine cause-and-effect relationships between certain behaviors and good and bad health, the questions become even more complicated.

V   Driving with Sensors

Many new cars today come with GPS and other in-car navigation schemes as well as with external cameras (to help for parallel parking and backing up), sensors that determine proximity to other cars, and remote control of locks and ignition. In some cases, these systems allow police to quickly track down a stolen car and even to kill the ignition remotely.

As cars become more computerized, it's reasonable to expect that sensors providing general feedback of driving habits will be included in some models. In fact, today it's easy to buy and install a GPS-based tracking system to monitor driving.[18] And some insurance companies use in-car sensors to gauge the safe driving of drivers who volunteer for such systems, adjusting the insurance premiums accordingly.

Conventional auto insurance rewards drivers based on their previous experience. A driver is deemed "safe" based on a number of considerations: the number of traffic violations on record, her age, and the type of car she drives, to name just a few factors.

Lately, however, there's been an option for a different model of automobile insurance called "pay-as-you-drive" (PAYD).

Instead of waiting until a person has a record of safe or unsafe driving, a PAYD scheme uses continuous feedback of a person's driving habits. In its simplest form, a PAYD system uses the odometer of a car, reducing premiums for drivers who drive less frequently. But in-car sensors that transmit data—about speed, distance, time of day driven, and sometimes GPS—back to insurance companies provide more data and more accurate data. Such systems let insurers adjust rates according to a range of behaviors such as speeding, driving too long, or driving in crime-prone neighborhoods much more frequently.

A number of companies in the United States—including Progressive, Liberty Mutual, MileMeter, and General Motors Acceptance Corporation (GMAC)—use PAYD schemes, and a few companies in the United Kingdom, Canada, South Africa, and Japan offer some PAYD options as well. At least 30 US states allow a PAYD option, but uptake has been slower abroad due to a lack of demand.

The state of California, for example, pushed PAYD insurance legislation in 2009. In addition to reducing premiums for some drivers, a PAYD system might also provide an incentive for people to drive less, thus reducing emission of greenhouse gasses. By some estimates, even a 30 percent adoption of PAYD insurance schemes nationwide could result in a 10 percent reduction in miles driven—a reduction of 55 million tons of carbon dioxide emissions over 10 years.

In the original California proposal, insurance companies could have required that customers install electronic monitoring equipment on their car. For insurance companies, this approach reduces the chance of fraud from simply relying on a car's odometer, which can easily be adjusted. But the Electronic Frontier Foundation, a nonprofit digital-rights advocacy and legal organization, pressured lawmakers to revise the bill to include both odometer readings and readings from electronic monitors.

The fear surrounding such PAYD programs is that insurance companies might sell or otherwise share personal information with other organizations or governments and that they might be prone to breeches in security. In addition, customers could face challenges with audits if they suspect price gouging. For instance, electronic monitoring systems could rely on a number of variables, including speed, location, driving time, and drive distance and frequency to determine premiums. The algorithms that weigh the importance of each variable could be hidden behind intellectual property rights, keeping a person from being able to vet the integrity of her premium. And finally, the metric alone might not tell the whole story about a driver's safe driving. A driver who exceeds the speed limit occasionally might, in fact, drive more safely than one who is slower and hesitates in traffic.

So although a smarter set of sensors and algorithms in cars could lead to finding stolen cars faster and reducing premiums for certain drivers, it undoubtedly complicates privacy policies and legislative action, ultimately putting some drivers in a compromised and vulnerable position.

VI   Watching the Watchers

Each year more people voluntarily put streams of their data exhaust online, be it workout routes, throwaway thoughts, or pictures of their children. Although those who post online may not constantly consider the potential uses of their public data, they have made the decision to do so and are, in most cases, able to remove their data from public view.

The case is very different for an elderly person or someone who has limited mental or physical functionality. The people in these groups generally don't have much say in the implementation of systems that monitor their position or behaviors. As a result, they must put trust in those who watch them and their monitoring systems.

Some people have a fundamental ethical problem with the idea of tagging the elderly or people with limited functionality: At stake is basic human dignity.[19] When a caretaker or doctor decides that a person must be tagged and tracked, that person's autonomy is diminished, making it easier to overlook his or her basic civil liberties.

On top of these civil liberties considerations in general, it's certainly not unheard of to find caretakers who cross ethical lines when dealing with their patients. Unfortunately, not all caretakers watch kindly. Cases of caretaker abuse and financial exploitation are becoming more common in parts of the United States.[20] This increase has prompted federal lawmakers to develop bills that require more stringent background checks for caretakers, among other provisions to try to limit elder abuse. However, it's unclear if more stringent background checks will help in an estimated 90 percent of cases in which the abuser is a family member who might not have a history of caretaking to check.[21]

At the same time, technology is allowing elderly people and those with limited functionality to live independently longer, with caretakers doing their work remotely. General Electric, for example, has a product in which ubiquitous sensors can accurately and unobtrusively determine an independent elderly person's activity. Currently, simple tracking systems are more common, such as a GPS-programmed "geofence" that sends an alert to a caretaker if the person has left a predefined area. The device is targeted to people who suffer from Alzheimer's disease, although it can be used with children and teenagers as well.[22]

Lawmakers should be more aware of the possibility of caretakers abusing devices such as the i-TAG and the more sophisticated sensor systems. If an abused person leaves his or her home to escape, the caretaker would be notified instantly. And if gadgets or software monitor call logs as well, an abused person might have even more limited recourse.

The abusive caretaker situation resembles, in some ways, the much more common occurrence of domestic violence and even electronic stalking by a stranger. It's a relatively straightforward task to install a tracking device on a person's car without her knowledge. And in at least one case, a victim of domestic abuse has sued the gadgetmaker, Foxtrax Vehicle Tracking, for aiding and abetting her abuser in an attack.[23]

The police are also using personal GPS tracking on the other side of the domestic violence battle: more states are using GPS to keep track of people with restraining orders against them,[24] a tactic that law enforcement has previously used to keep track of people convicted of sexually abusing children.[25]

VII Conclusion

Although it's clear that applications that use a person's data can help him live a more productive life, exercise more, or kick a smoking habit and in themselves can be useful and exciting, they can't exist without the accompanying questions of privacy. Researchers try to envision a world in which these applications have existed for decades, and so they often put out the call for a more in-depth "conversation" about the questions that need to be asked and the implications that inevitably arise with such technologies. However, it's still often the case that the privacy concerns regarding or vulnerabilities within a new technology, be it a GPS-based phone application or RFID-based toll tag, emerge only after the technology has been adopted and started to cause problems.

One of the most popular ways of addressing concerns is by allowing people to opt in or opt out of programs or technologies. However, in some cases it's not feasible to opt out entirely. Therefore, there need to be various approaches to data collection and analysis that offer a range of privacy options. Included with each privacy setting should be clear, concise explanations of the ramifications of that setting. For instance, many people allow mobile phone applications to use their location if the application asks, but few people are fully aware of how those data are used and shared.

Attitudes toward privacy are continually evolving, as anyone who has blithely posted a picture on Facebook or a sentiment on Twitter can attest; the line between private lives and public lives has been blurring for years. Those pictures and words are visible to anyone who uses a web browser and search engine. The forthcoming batch of technologies that uses personal data, whether those data are publicly visible or not, will likely be able to take advantage of public consensus (or at least fatigue) that in many cases reduce the "friction" in collecting and making use of personal data for various applications.

These are exciting times for individuals to use Reality-Mining approaches to transform data into improved habits and health and to save some money. As the ideas around personal Big Data become more prevalent and more valuable to the general public, varied discussions by policymakers, activists, and technologists over data ownership and the legality of certain data-based products will arise. Now's the time to take seriously the consequences of data-based products such as those mentioned earlier. If implemented correctly, such products could provide positive examples for those that follow.

II The Neighborhood and the Organization (10 to 1,000 People)

3 Gathering Data from Small Heterogeneous Groups

As chapter 1 illustrated, there is an abundance of inexpensive commercial ways to log an individual person's data. The methods are relatively straightforward, and a person can in some ways control how her data are being used and how that use benefits her. But the complexity of collecting data and of providing appropriate incentives for collection increase when personal data are gathered within small groups of people, even if those people share a common allegiance or goal.

Whereas collecting personal data for personal analytics feels contained and private, collecting personal data to share even with a small group of people can make those within the group feel vulnerable or exposed. And at the next level, small-group data collection, in which a person's identity may be explicitly tied to her data, is quite different from that of data collection in large groups (generally more than 10,000 people), where identifying information is often stripped from the data, giving a sense of anonymity.

When considering specific use cases, such as use by companies or neighborhood organizations, particular challenges arise. People instinctively balk when a boss or other authority figure has access to detailed personal information. Likewise, data gathering at the neighborhood level is also difficult: the people who use personal neighborhood data—city planners, politicians, or community organizers—might not have the support of everyone in the area, leading to spotty voluntary participation.

Therefore, most of the efforts at this scale of data collection have been confined to research projects in which participants have signed on to share their data willingly. These projects, therefore, have a certain homogeneity to them, and they are often conducted on college campuses, where people share certain traits or behaviors. The original 2003 Reality-Mining study outlined in chapter 1, for instance, was completed with 100 participants, all students at MIT.

Although some commercial attempts have been made to devise ways to collect behavioral data from people at the small-group scale, these approaches have been slow to catch on. One example is "smart" conference badges that use RFID or infrared sensors to discern social networks based on the conference participants' communication patterns. Such smart badges offer an easy way to share contact information and for conference organizers to track attendance of sessions. Although these smart badges have been around for years, they still aren't widely used, due in part to cost and issues with reliability and usability.

In the workplace, there's no shortage of software that provides a way to store and mine data from workers, including content produced, websites visited, and emails sent. Known as "knowledge-management systems," these software tools promise to improve worker efficiency, collaboration, and communication by allowing workers easier access to information or "knowledge" within their organizations. Knowledge-management tools have found limited success, however, due to difficulty in integrating them into a company's technical and social culture.

"Knowledge" is often added to a system, but not until after it would be useful for a particular project. In addition, knowledge-management tools can be expensive to maintain and difficult to scale in a timely way.

Other types of workplace monitoring come from key-swipe monitors, analytics from work-related phone conversations (words, tone, frequency, etc.), and sensors to track movement around an office or facility. These tools are almost never employed—the notable exception being call centers, where phone calls are often monitored—for obvious reasons. Few companies are willing to risk alienating employees or, worse, precipitating legal action in an attempt to improve workplace efficiency in this unproven way.

Outside of companies and the workplace, researchers have found a number of interesting reasons to collect data at the neighborhood scale. Projects on and around college campuses rely on citizen participation to explore various aspects of the environment, from air pollution and garbage piles to road conditions and commuting routes. The collection is straightforward, often using mobile phones as sensors, but the challenge comes in expanding the range of the projects outside of academic settings. One key component to expanding beyond academia is providing the most appropriate incentives to allow people to make informed decisions about the trade-off between sharing their personal data within a small group and receiving some type of benefit from it.

Perhaps the most obvious incentive is to provide people with smart phones as well as data and voice plans in exchange for their data. A few years ago one company, Integrated Media Measurement, Inc. (IMMI), was successful in persuading people to share audio snippets of their lives with the company in exchange for a

smart phone. IMMI's goal was to use the audio sample to determine the sort of media—radio, television, or movie, for example—that a person is consuming. This information can be used
to compile information about the popularity of certain media
content, much like Neilson's media survey system. Notably, the
technology doesn't log and store personal conversations or even
raw data. Even so, such a project would have an extremely difficult time being approved by a university's ethics committee and
institutional review board because it wouldn't be permissible to
collect audio data from people who did not sign a consent form
to participate in the study, which would be a necessary byprod-
uct of audio data collection from primary subjects.[1]

This chapter explores the technical, legal, and sociological
challenges that researchers and companies face when trying to
collect data nonanonymously from groups of people. Why have
some approaches succeeded where others have failed? And what
are the opportunities available at this scale of Reality Mining?

I Conference Connections

Conferences and events are fertile grounds for collecting a variety of personal information. When people register, they supply
a certain amount of demographic information, and when they
attend, they often want to maximize the number and quality
of social connections they make. A smart badge that tracks personal interactions and that can provide people with, at a minimum, an electronic contact list seems like a useful improvement
over traditional hand shaking and card swapping.

Smart conference badges range in design and function and
in the way they collect and store data. At the basic end, they are
equipped with an RFID chip. The chip contains a small amount

of identifying information and can be read by specialized readers either at close range or at a distance of meters. Most often, RFID conference badges are used to track attendance of sessions and meals. But in some cases they are used to track movement of participants and proximity to various readers, often located at vendors' booths. These badges transmit identifying information to electronic RFID readers at certain locations, which in turn access applications, often on remote servers, to analyze the data.

These RFID-enabled badges often closely resemble traditional badges in appearance and are just as lightweight. Price is still a barrier, however. Although the cost of manufacturing RFID chips has fallen over the past decade, smart badges are still more expensive compared to traditional ones. Companies such as Microsoft and IBM have used RFID badges at conferences experimentally,[2] and a few companies, such as Alliance Tech and Convention Strategy, have commercialized them. These commercial badges are able to track the amount of time people spend looking at a display or a booth and can send email and text message alerts to people at conference booths when attendees with certain profiles—those who have certain job titles or who work at specific companies—enter the range of the reader.

One major issue with these badges is the lack of privacy controls. When a person wears this badge, his data are visible to RFID readers at all times unless he physically blocks the signal with a conductive material such as aluminum foil. The fact that people can't choose what an RFID reader sees and which RFID readers can see it creates a situation in which the wearer has a lack of control and might therefore be less likely to wear the tag—a hurdle if this sort of technology is to become more widely adopted.

At the other end of the smart badge spectrum are electronic badges that use multiple sensors as well as RFID to let people share contact information and interact with their own as well as with others' badges. These badges can come with a simple interface and with a display and buttons that allow people to see data and answer survey questions on the device, for instance.

This interactivity is a huge advantage over simple RFID badges because a person can choose the type of information she wants transmitted, which improves her sense of control, thereby increasing her comfort with sharing data. During the MIT Reality-Mining study, participants were given the option to "go stealth" if at any time they didn't want their phones to collect data on their behavior. The option for a stealth mode calmed participants' fears about the collection of their personal data, including the people they mingled with in and out of school. Participants reported being pleased to have control over their data, but during the course of the study few participants actually activated the stealth mode.

Due to their relative complexity, sensor-laden electronic badges are more expensive than RFID badges, which is a major impediment to broader adoption. In addition, they tend to be heavier, which can make them awkward to wear all day and over multiple days at a conference.

One notable company in this space is the MIT spinout nTag. In March 2009, Alliance Tech acquired nTag, hired key staff, and now is the exclusive provider of nTag technology.[3] Among other features, the nTag badge was capable of prompting wearers to engage in conversations with others, to exchange business cards electronically, and to communicate easily with staff, speakers, and attendees. Similar to RFID-only badges, the nTag badge could also let conference organizers monitor attendance of sessions and booths.

It's unclear how these badge companies will fare in an era when more and more people have smart phones capable of many of the functions that the badges provide. It might perhaps be an economical option to hire a developer to build apps for some of the major smart phone operating systems so that attendees can replicate on their own personal devices the sort of functions that are available on an nTag badge.

II   Eye on Employees

Companies famous for their data-mining software, such as Oracle and IBM, have for years deployed techniques to analyze terabytes of data produced by employees. The primary purpose of this mining, called "knowledge management," is to streamline transactions, develop effective marketing campaigns, identify fraud, optimize sales, and capture something called "eDiscovery," which law firms use to build court cases. The ultimate goal is to improve the workplace by increasing worker productivity and, ideally, worker satisfaction.

One prominent company in this space was Tacit Software, a firm founded in 1997 and acquired by Oracle in 2008. Tacit developed software (explained in more detail in chapter 4) that was able to analyze email communications, blogs, and wikis to determine people's interests and expertise. Used by companies such as Lockheed Martin, Northrop Grumman, and GlaxoSmithKline, the software was able to facilitate introductions between people in large companies who could help each other solve pressing problems.

Another company, Declara, is currently operating as a so-called virtual consultancy and collaboration platform. Its software is able to create a social network across people in an organization and with the data they produce find the best matches between individuals and the information they seek.

Although Tacit's and Declara's technology is highly proprietary, there are other less-expensive open-source options. For example, OpenKM is available for all major operating systems and allows files to be stored in local file systems or database-management systems such as Oracle and MySQL.[4] In addition, there are numerous open-source software tools that deal with aspects of knowledge management, including KOAN Ontology and Semantic Web Infrastructure, Exteca, Haystack, and Kowari, to name a few.[5]

As well as revealing expertise and interest, employee-created data can also provide insight into the productivity of people within an organization. In the past couple of years, human-resource departments at companies have embraced using employee-created data to evaluate worker efficiency. It's still a new practice, but it could provide a way for employers to quantitatively evaluate an employee's productivity as well as his role and effectiveness in the company's worker network.[6]

One company, Cataphora, is now leveraging technology that it previously developed to legally prove that companies had committed fraud in order to help companies today determine whether employees themselves are committing crimes. The software monitors employees' electronic transactions, including emails, attachments sent and received, instant messages, and calendar appointments. It finds patterns of communication and exceptions to patterns—such as unusual language used to sign off, sometimes a sign of fraud.[7] The software can unearth employee cliques, potentially giving human-resource specialists clues to the groups of people who work productively and those who don't. In addition to offering enterprise-grade software, the company also offers a book and commercial software for an employee so he can get a sense of how his employers might interpret his personal data.

Although it's true that a significant portion of an office worker's day is spent sending and receiving electronic communications, there are other indicators of productivity and social interaction that can be looked at as well. For instance, electronic ID card records can reveal a person's movement throughout the day.

In addition, text messages, phone calls, and recordings of calls can be used to evaluate employees' social networks and behaviors. Call centers are notorious for monitoring phone calls to try to optimize the interactions that employees have with customers. Software can now extract features that provide companies a sense of customer sentiment on these calls. The company Verint Systems Inc. integrates speech analytics with other input such as text from email and instant messages and responses from surveys to get a more complete picture of a customer's experience with a company.[8]

Beyond industries that use call centers, it's uncommon for employers to monitor audio from the phone calls that employees make. Yet complete recording of workers' conversations might not be necessary to gain insight into a company's social networks and into the possible productivity of individual and groups of employees. Analysis of audio features such as turn-taking style and rate of speed in face-to-face conversations has been used to determine the structure of social networks.[9] Extending this sort of analysis to phone calls without recording entire conversations could provide benefits while minimizing privacy concerns.

Legality is a legitimate concern in this space, especially because laws are not well established that firmly protect either employees or employers. Although it is legal to record all business-related phone calls, in most cases this monitoring must be announced to both parties. Personal calls, if determined to be personal, may not be monitored. However, if an employee has been told not to make personal calls at work, he takes a risk that the call may be monitored.[10]

In June 2010, the Supreme Court unanimously decided in *City of Ontario v. Quon* (130 S.Ct. 2619, 560 U.S.) that it is legal to search the messages on a police officer's government-owned pager based on work-related grounds.[11] In this case, the city was trying to determine whether to modify its wireless contract based on usage and so obtained a transcript of Quon's messages, which turned out to be sexually explicit.[12] The decision invoked the Fourth Amendment regarding government intrusion into electronic communication of public employees. Although the case and decision might have influenced the space of government-employee privacy, it is not conclusive in cases where the employer is private.

There is a possibility that employees would be more receptive to a sort of surveillance by their employers if the analysis of the data were tied to benefits or pay increases. One important feature of such a system would be transparency: the methods used to collect and analyze data are made clear, and its conclusions are open to refutation and appeal. Much like the health-incentive system mentioned in chapter 2, the results of a proposed employee-surveillance system should be used only to incentivize people, not penalize them.

This is easier said than done, however, and disparities in raises and salaries are often points of contention within organizations, more so than the cost of health care per employee. In addition, analysis of such employee data is much more complex than the straightforward approach that most health-incentive systems use. For example, in the latter, if a person walks x amount of steps a month, he will pay x amount less for health insurance than he would otherwise. One of the best ways to improve worker productivity is to improve workplace satisfaction, but if an employer appears to encroach on workers' rights and privacy, the entire operation could backfire.

III Neighborhood Improvement

When considering data collection around neighborhoods, entirely different sets of challenges and opportunities arise. These projects often rely on a fairly homogenous group of people, such as university students or professors, and data collection is limited to geographies around universities. However, these projects point to possible applications and incentive schemes for broader participation. Researchers and some companies have been tapping into people's desires to create a more livable community— an approach that in some cases is fairly effective in overcoming reluctance to share personal data.

One emerging application explored by research labs at Intel and the University of California is to map pollution tracked by personal, portable air-quality sensors.[13] The project, called Common Sense, collects data on personal exposure as well as aggregate exposure of groups of people. By tapping into people's desire to improve their own health and the health of their environment, the researchers were able to persuade participants to share location traces from their mobile phones as well as data from participant-worn sensor packs that track carbon monoxide, nitrogen oxides, and ozone gas as well as light, temperature, humidity, and orientation in space. The results of such collection could help activists mobilize community action accordingly.

Expanding such an application to a broader audience might be years away, however. The major challenge is the lack of mass-market demand for the integration of most of the environmental sensors into mobile phones. In addition, there's a challenge with the "cleanliness" of the data, which depends upon the conditions under which the phones collect it. Commercial attempts at this sort of data collection will therefore most likely need to use inexpensive, unobtrusive external sensors that have a Bluetooth radio to communicate with a user's mobile device.

A number of projects from the University of California at Los Angeles (UCLA) group led by Deborah Estrin have explored these sort of mobile phone–only approaches to data collection in neighborhoods. As it happens, mobile phones, equipped with cameras and GPS, lend themselves well to many neighborhood-improvement possibilities. In fact, ideas that incorporate some of the UCLA project's parameters are now finding their way to the masses as start-ups are creating similar mobile phone apps.

One project, Personalized Environmental Impact Report, uses location data, securely and regularly uploaded to remote servers, to provide a report of environmental impact and exposure.[14] By analyzing a user's location trace and data from thousands of neighborhoods in California—such as weather conditions and estimated traffic patterns—the system creates a report that provides estimates of the participant's exposure to smog levels and the number of fast-food restaurants he encountered. It also estimates a person's carbon impact and his impact on sensitive sites such as schools and hospitals, which can be affected by cars being driven by them, for instance.

Another UCLA project that illustrates the potential benefits of people sharing data at the neighborhood level uses mobile phones to report instances of loose garbage on a college campus. For the project, college students were encouraged to take pictures with mobile phones of contents of campus garbage bins to help determine where recycle bins could be placed most effectively.

Mobile phones are also being used at UCLA to help find better bike-commuting paths. The project Biketastic[15] collects GPS traces of bike commuters' routes as well as accelerometer data to document the roughness of the road and audio data that could help determine traffic conditions or construction on the route. When combined with other data sets, including air quality, time-sensitive traffic data, and traffic accidents, a full picture of the quality of a bike commute route becomes clear.

IV Soundscape Surveillance

As evident by the UCLA projects, the myriad sensors on a phone allow it to be the ultimate environmental observer. But a simple, continuously collected audio profile of an environment can be powerful as well. In 2010, Arbitron Inc. acquired the technology portfolio, patents, and trade name of IMMI, now known as Audience Measurement Technologies, Inc. IMMI used ambient audio to provide insight into the type of media people are consuming. Competing directly with Nielson Media Research, IMMI had been trying to get a picture of all forms of media, from movies, radio, and games to MP3s, television, and the Web. The technology used to do this was an audio recorder that ran on a smart phone and on a personal computer. The recorder captured snippets of sound several times a minute and matched signatures of sound in a database. The technology worked without the help of a user, thus providing an unbiased sample of a person's soundscape. It could provide real-time reports on an individual's listening habits that were cross-referenced with a person's demographic information, provided when he or she signed up for the service.

More than 10,000 people agreed to use IMMI's technology. Although this size of group technically puts IMMI's technology outside this chapter's small-group scope, the basic method of data collection—on the client side rather than on the server side—and the fact that data are tied directly to an identified individual as opposed to an anonymous person or group average make it a good fit for collecting data from a relatively small group of people.

When a person decided to use IMMI's technology, he would download it to his phone or personal computer or accept an IMMI-provided smart phone preloaded with the data-collection technology. Every few minutes, his device would collect an audio sample. Audio was immediately converted to digital signatures, which were then sent to the company's servers. Media were identified when the collected digital signatures were matched with signatures on the servers computed by IMMI from monitored media, target content files, commercials, promos, movies, and songs. The process of matching took only a few seconds.

In terms of privacy, the company claimed that conversations and other nonmedia sounds were simply filtered out. Because the audio was immediately converted to a digital signature, and the signature was matched to preidentified media content, there was no reason or method to analyze other audio, including conversations and street sounds. And there was likely an important incentive at play: IMMI offered a subsidized device and service to those who accepted the phone preloaded with software. For some people, at least, this was enough of an incentive to quiet their qualms about a technology that might appear to listen in on their lives.

IMMI's technology is now part of Arbitron, which developed the Portable People Meter, a pager-size device dedicated to detecting inaudible tones embedded in broadcast signal. When these signals are detected, they are wirelessly transmitted to Arbitron's servers. The Portable People Meter is currently deployed in Canada, Iceland, Norway, Sweden, Denmark, Belgium, and Kazakhstan, and the audio-encoding technology has been licensed in Singapore.

V   Conclusion

In the case of small groups of people, the biggest challenge of data collection is finding the right incentives for people to participate, especially in the case in which people are easily and directly connected with the data they produce. Smart conference badges may be held back due to economics, but workplaces and neighborhoods have the potential to use Reality-Mining technology to get a better handle on how people actually work and behave. And if the benefits of sharing data with a community can be effectively communicated and demonstrated, it's likely more people would accept certain terms of data sharing.

IMMI hit on a way to get people to share the intimate details of their environmental audio: it offered free smart phones and promised that personal conversations would be excluded. But perhaps further analysis of the cost–benefit of sharing personal data should be done. In one study, in particular, it was found that students were willing to share location data (collected by their mobile phones) for a median compensation of £10.

Students who traveled away from the university more often valued their privacy more and, as a result, requested more compensation than those who stayed close to campus.[16] This study indicates that people do assign value to their personal location data and that this value varies based on such factors as mobility.

Researchers and businesspeople need to be more aware of the value of a person's data and compensate accordingly. It's a tricky scale to operate within, given inherent privacy concerns, but it's one in which the possibility of rich applications await those who can do it conscientiously.

4 Engineering and Policy: Building More Efficient Businesses, Enabling Hyperlocal Politics, Life Queries, and Opportunity Searches

Just as chapter 2 outlines the various ways a single person's data can be harnessed to build systems and tools to help her achieve goals or live a healthier life, this chapter shows how small-group data can be used to improve individual productivity and health, facilitate more useful group interactions, and build healthier, more livable communities. With small-group data, engineers have the potential to easily identify meaningful and casual relationships between people, events, and their environment that can help workplace managers, citizen activists, health-care providers, and local government officials make better decisions.

At this scale, social network alliances and hierarchies become clear and can help explain group behavior. But these insights are most relevant when they are actionable—leading to organizations that run smoother or neighborhoods that are better to live in. Therefore, it is important not to constrain the scope of this work to mere observational science; designing better organizations and neighborhoods fundamentally comes down to engineering. The challenge, of course, is to engineer systems with the correct mix of incentives so people feel comfortable sharing data they have created and unthreatened by certain parties' access to it.

Happily, a number of companies and researchers are developing applications to do just that. Knowledge-brokering systems, such as those made by Tacit, discussed in chapter 3, analyze employees' work and communication behavior, helping them to make new connections with each other. Similar principles have been applied to facilitating introductions in a conference or dating setting, using a mobile phone application known as Serendipity. But the key is to ensure everyone's privacy and agency—building a system that only facilitates rather than forces introductions without compromising an individual's privacy or security.

Moving from data in the workplace to data in the neighborhood, it is possible to begin to leverage data from relatively small groups of local citizens interested in improving quality of life at the neighborhood level. Participatory sensing projects from UCLA, also discussed in chapter 3, allow citizens to monitor pollution levels, an application that highlights which paths are the most safe for asthma sufferers, for instance.

But even more interesting are the sort of participatory sensing projects that have come out of labs as commercial projects, extended to thousands of people. In one example, Project Noah (Networked Organisms and Habitats), a New York University spinout, enables citizen scientists to record geotagged and time-stamped pictures of and notes about organisms they observe, thus providing snapshots of a local ecosystem's health over time. CitySourced, another mobile phone application, lets people send geotagged and time-stamped pictures of blight to their respective city halls. CitySourced is one of a number of applications becoming available and integrated into city workflow systems and city 311 (nonemergency) resources that let people directly share data they have personally collected with city workers who can solve the problem being shown.

The value to the community derived from these local participatory sensing systems would be impossible without contributions from a subset of the local population—the people who have been successfully incentivized by the system to provide potentially sensitive information. As the mechanisms that incentivize this sharing become increasingly better engineered, they will begin to play an even greater role in shaping and maintaining the places where we work and live.

This chapter looks at the potential of these local applications, including techniques that designers can use to persuade people to participate while protecting their privacy. In some cases, the incentives are a clear gain in productivity or cooperation, and private data to a third party do not have to be relinquished. In other cases, designers are integrating elements of gaming into their applications so people feel a sense of accomplishment when they participate. When the benefits are clear and privacy is maintained, people become increasingly willing to share personal data in ways that make their workplaces and neighborhoods better for themselves and for their colleagues and neighbors.

I   Social Network Interventions: Tie Creation

Tacit Software, a company that branded its software as a knowledge-brokering system, collects intimate details from emails sent by an organization's members. These details—recipients of emails, content of attachments, and words within an email itself—are used to infer employees' social networks, knowledge, and interests. Because Tacit's type of data collection could make many employees uneasy, the software was engineered around strict and transparent privacy controls. All information is encrypted, which means that it is impossible for anyone at

the organization, including the information technology direc-
tors and the CEO, to see the analysis of an individual's interests
and social ties. It's also impossible for anyone at Tacit to access
this information. Only with a court order will Tacit divulge this
sensitive data, and accessing it requires keys from both Tacit and
the company who uses the system.

So how does it work? The software reveals relationship information only when all parties explicitly authorize it. For example, imagine that Roger suspects that a project he's working on
relates to other projects within his company, but he doesn't
know which ones or who might be working on them. Roger
could email a number of different people, describing his project and asking if they're aware of something similar and, if so,
whether they would mind introducing Roger to someone who
could further explain the similar project. Or he could query
the knowledge-brokering system. The system, which continuously discovers who is associated with various topics and projects, would privately ask matching people if they would like to
be introduced to Roger for the purpose of discussing the project. Although Roger made his identity explicit by initiating the
search, only those who accept the system's offer are actually
introduced to him. Those who ignore the offer from the system,
if any, remain anonymous.

The idea is to facilitate the sharing of knowledge, interests,
and relationships to increase workplace efficiency. Systems that
facilitate the creation of new relationships are a compliment
to traditional knowledge-management systems in which docu-
ments are analyzed and cataloged and taxonomies are created.
The trouble with these traditional knowledge-management systems is that they are usually one step behind the actual creation
of knowledge and relationships. Automated systems such as

Tacit's are able to unearth expertise and relationships when they matter to the people who need to use them, while preserving the ability of those holding the data to keep them private if they so choose.

The 2004 MIT project Serendipity[1] is similar to Tacit in the way that it brokers introductions through an outside system. Using data collected on participants' mobile phones, just as in the original MIT Reality-Mining project, Serendipity attempted to bring together strangers who share similar interests when they are in relatively close physical proximity to each other. Although the original idea was to use Serendipity to mediate interactions at large companies or conferences, the idea was also spun out into a mobile dating company called MetroSpark.

MetroSpark asked users to provide data about themselves for their registration profile and to weigh those interests according to importance. It used this information and the weights to calculate "similarity scores." If users gave their permission, MetroSpark could also glean more implicit user information from behaviors inferred by software on their phones, such as their sleeping schedule, common hangouts, relationships, and even the use of games or other applications on the phone. In addition, users could also provide information about the types of people they wanted to be introduced to. All of this information made up a user's profile, which was stored on a central server.

When the similarity score of two users was above the threshold set by both users who were within Bluetooth range of each other, the server alerted the users that there was someone in their proximity who might be of interest. As a privacy consideration and social courtesy, the system would alert the users by sending a text message to ask if they would be interested in meeting someone with similar interests. If both users responded "yes," the system would then send a picture and a list of talking points to both phones.

Similar to MetroSpark, other geosocial apps—such as Grindr, a mobile dating app targeted to gay men, and Blendr, a mobile app targeted to introducing people across a range of demographics—allow users to upload photos and profiles. Blendr, for instance, lets a person scan nearby profiles (exact location is obscured) and tag profiles of interest. A person can see who has tagged her Blendr profile. If a person has tagged her and she has also tagged his or her profile, then both users can chat directly through the app.[2]

Unfortunately, not all software developers have considered two-party consent in building their apps. Girls Around Me is an example of a consent-free app that easily enabled anonymous and sometimes predatory behavior. The app, made for iPhones, linked public information from Facebook profiles with real-time location information from Foursquare, putting it all on an easily searchable map. Without asking permission, the app lets a user search an area and see pictures, relationship status, interests, and exact location of people who had provided this information online, but who might not have been aware that all such information was publicly available. In essence, the app combined details from people's profiles and their exact locations unbeknownst to them and without their explicit permission, so in 2012 the app was pulled from the Apple Store. Foursquare also denied the Girls Around Me access to its application programming interface (API), citing a policy that disallows aggregation of information across venues to prevent an inappropriate overview of a series of locations.[3]

With the Girls Around Me app, developers took advantage of the fact that Facebook's privacy terms are often updated by the company and are sometimes confusing to use, which leaves some people's profile information unexpectedly exposed. MetroSpark, Tacit, Grindr, and Blendr, in contrast, rely on users' explicit confirmation in order to share identifying information or to broker an introduction. Nevertheless, these services exist in a privacy gray area that still makes many reasonable people uncomfortable enough to never use them. It's a space where design must be carefully considered and transparency is paramount to broader adoption.

II Taking Note of the Neighborhood

At this scale of data collection, some of the biggest advantages can come from sharing location along with even just one other piece of data collected from a sensor, such as a camera or accelerometer. When members of a neighborhood collect these "covariates" and map them to a particular location, they can potentially bring to light hidden features of their neighborhood, which has the potential to help improve the quality of life for everyone. This type of neighborhood data collection also has a distinct advantage over collecting data at companies: you don't need to convince everyone to participate in order to get useful information, unlike the process for an organization, where a complete social graph is ideal.

Project Noah[4] lets people take geotagged and time-stamped pictures of plants, animals, and fungi and upload them to an online database of organisms. The website provides a searchable map, and future iterations of the application will allow people to create their own neighborhood ecosystem so students in classes or local bird-watchers can have an easier way to see local information. Users are motivated by participating in certain "missions" that focus on collecting pictures and information about a specific species and by earning virtual patches—much like merit badges—based on contributions.

Project Noah links physical communities and online communities, providing insight into the ecological health of an area over time. The data are currently being used by hobbyists as well as by scientists at the University of Illinois at Chicago and Cornell University to supplement data for projects on squirrels[5] and ladybugs,[6] respectively. The data can also be used to keep tabs on endangered species and to track the progress of invasive species, which are indicators of an ecosystem's overall health.

Where Project Noah focuses on the ecological health of a community, a number of mobile apps are letting people report the health of the man-made side of their neighborhoods. CitySourced, SeeClickFix, FixMyStreet, and a handful of other mobile apps allow people to send geotagged, time-stamped, and precategorized photos to their city government. In some cases, these apps connect directly to a city's back-office workflow systems and produce work orders or route complaints to police departments automatically, which means that fixing a pothole or cleaning up graffiti can happen more quickly and efficiently.

It doesn't take much to convince city managers, chief information officers, and mayors to support these sorts of initiatives. What's good for the city's citizens is good for politics. And the most successful of these apps are made by companies interested in tightly integrating their software to a city's existing infrastructure, so no expensive information technology changes are necessary.

In fact, some city governments are taking the lead, developing apps themselves. In California, San Jose's "San Jose 311" system was built by CitySourced and effectively launched the small company's business.[7] Likewise, the city of San Francisco is simply opening access to some of its data—street-cleaning schedules, park information, and information about recycling facilities—to foster the development of any mobile apps or websites that provide a useful way to share the city's information.

And it is only becoming easier for cities and app developers to work together thanks to an initiative called Open311, facilitated by the New York City–based nonprofit OpenPlans. The goal is to create an open platform that allows cities to leverage their preexisting infrastructure for distributing city information so that it's easier to develop websites and mobile apps.[8]

At this point, most of these services allow users to report urban blight anonymously, sharing only their location with the service. Because the payoff—a cleaner neighborhood—can be achieved with only sporadic location information from individual users, many people feel comfortable using it. Future versions of these mobile apps, however, may give users the option to register and provide more personal information. This option might allow users to more easily receive updates about their complaints, be informed about community action, and participate in games and contests.

Another way that mobile phones can help improve a community's health is in allowing people to share their running, cycling, and commuting routes with others in the area. Since the mid-2000s, a number of websites have offered user-generated running and cycling routes that can be searched by location and distance. Mapmyrun.com, Mapmyride.com, Walkjogrun.net, bikely, Runkeeper, Runtastic, and DailyMile.com are commonly used for sharing and finding routes. The data for these routes can be either manually entered or uploaded from a GPS device. Many of these apps easily allow a person to share a route from an activity trace recorded on an iPhone or Android device.

There's still quite a bit of untapped potential, however, for easily searchable bike-commuting routes, a problem to which a neighborhood crowdsourcing solution—in which a group of people contribute data or resources to solve a problem—is well suited. Bike commuters tend to be motivated to share their tips and tactics with others who are considering alternatives to car commuting, but currently there's no easy way to find acceptable routes to downtown areas from various neighborhoods that include information about rush-hour traffic or road conditions (the sort of data collected from cyclists in the UCLA project Biketastic, mentioned in chapter 3).

In addition, estimated time of travel, at a leisurely pace, with stoplights could be helpful for new bike commuters. Popular services such as Runkeeper and DailyMile would do well to include a search function specifically for commuters. And developers could make an app that would automatically collect information about a bike commute and upload it to these sites. In considering privacy, Runkeeper and DailyMile scrub the precise start and end point of a person's activity routes to provide a sense of security for those posting their routes online. Although there is no way to post a route anonymously, commuters wouldn't need to constantly share their commuting data with the public; sharing a route just once could provide valuable insight to others.

Tools that tap into the behavior of people in neighborhoods and correlate it to other data—such as traffic, air pollution, or other environmental indicators—could also be useful to activists. The University of California and Intel collaboration called Common Sense (described in chapter 3) points toward the possibility of outfitting people with air-quality sensors that send data to a mobile phone via Bluetooth. To effect change in communities, activists could provide air-quality sensors to people who use parks or wait at bus stops. If these sensors pick up high levels of pollutants, then there could be grounds for a campaign to petition local industries to reduce their hazardous emissions.

A recent innovative health-care project in Bayview, a predominantly low-income neighborhood in San Francisco that has long-suffered pollution from its proximity to the city's industrial sector, hopes to alleviate elements of a stressful environment that can lead to childhood and adult illnesses such as asthma, cancer, diabetes, and emphysema. These stressors include poor air quality and noise pollution, abuse, lack of healthy food, lack of exercise, and lack of social supports from family and other resources.[9]

Data from local children's mobile phones—about what routes they take to school, how long they wait for public transportation, proximity to grocery stores with fresh produce—could be an effective way to identify some systemic stressors in poor neighborhoods. Although pediatricians would not be able to solve all these problems using data from phones, they might suggest simple changes to their patients, such as taking a different route to school to reduce the amount of traffic they encounter or to make it more likely that they will walk past a market that sells fresh produce. In addition, mobile data could help health-care providers target neighborhoods with new recreational facilities and after-school resources. Although these sorts of interventions are fairly obvious even without information from mobile phones, hard data are persuasive, and they can be especially beneficial when correlating health-care interventions with health-care costs.

Long-term incentives for such programs might include future parks, recreation centers, and road diets in which traffic is slowed, sidewalks are widened, and greenery is planted. More direct and immediate incentives would include subsidizing part or all of participants' mobile phone subscriptions or services. Because families may rightfully be suspicious of a technology that keeps tabs on their children's location, program adoption throughout a community would also likely need to rely on influential community members who could introduce the technology and goals.

III Conclusion

As more data are produced and collected at the scale of small groups thanks to incentives and well-designed applications, there will likely be a shift away from academic theorizing and toward an evidence-based approach to the design of policies within the workplace and neighborhood. Although protocols and regulations are clearly needed to facilitate the appropriate and ethical use of small-group data and to protect individual privacy, the members of an organization or neighborhood have the right to benefit from the data they generate. It's clear that there are various opportunities at this scale if developers carefully consider motivation and user privacy.

When it comes to workplace productivity and efficiency, Tacit has found one of the most effective ways to ensure all users' privacy by acting only as a broker between people and information, allowing personal information to be shared only when an individual provides consent. In the case of reporting neighborhood blight by phone, people seem to be willing to share their anonymous location data with their city government. It remains to be seen if games or other incentives will motivate them to identify themselves; however, the growing number of people participating in the location application Foursquare and in features offered by Twitter and Facebook indicates that the public resistance to sharing location information is wearing down.

As applications that let people share commute, jog, or biking routes are becoming more popular, companies such as

Runkeeper and DailyMile need to carefully consider the type of safeguards that they can use to ensure that more people are sharing their data safely. These approaches to privacy and safety are applicable here because the data collected are sparse and the people who participate willingly opt in to a public database.

In the cases of pollution trackers and doctors who are trying to find stressors in communities by supplying mobile phones to patients, however, the privacy landscape shifts, and questions of ethics arise. Legal mechanisms might be needed to persuade participants that the data they share can't be used against them or given to others. Katie Shilton and Deborah Estrin of UCLA state the problem clearly: "If raw location data and experience sampling is too easily discoverable in civil litigation, individuals or entire demographics might be dissuaded from participation in this new form of investigation."[10] They suggest treating personal data in the same way that a noncommercial trade secret is treated, with something called evidentiary privilege. With this privilege, data can't be disclosed to certain parties, and they can't be subpoenaed or used in legal proceedings.

Discussions about the proprietary nature and protections of personal data are only now starting in earnest. Yet even without such protections, many people are still willing to share rich personal data such as location traces with companies that design apps and even post them publicly. They do so because they suspect the legal complications to be unlikely and the payoff of access to better information to be high. Therefore, it might be years before standards and laws are adopted that consider the nuances of this sort of data collection and sharing. In the meantime, the best practice is to simply and clearly inform people in all cases of the risks and benefits to sharing their data.

III   The City (1,000 to 1,000,000 People)

5 Traffic Data, Crime Stats, and Closed-Circuit Cameras: Accumulating Urban Analytics

As of 2009, more than half of the world's 7 billion people live in cities. In the United States, at least 82 percent of people are urbanites, whereas in the more rural India only 30 percent call a city home.[1] No matter the country, all cities generate a wealth of data that ultimately reflect the various behavior patterns of its diverse inhabitants. This chapter focuses on cities, defined here as 1,000 to about a million people and on two types of data that can in many ways define the rhythm of a city: traffic metrics and crime statistics.

Specifically, we explore the various ways in which traffic data are collected—crowdsourced from mobile phones and in-car GPS systems, from sensors on the road, and from traditional traffic reports by police and other roadway services—as well as their privacy and commercial implications. We also look at the proliferation of public crime databases that allow anyone, from cops and politicians to residents and real-estate agents, to take a look at where and when trouble strikes. In particular, this chapter examines all the challenges, both legal and technical, of collecting data via cameras, which are becoming more common for both traffic and crime monitoring.

Although the data-gathering techniques discussed in this chapter are for the most part straightforward, the implications of the data are wide ranging. Chapter 6 examines how knowledge of a city's traffic flow can help get resources to the roads that need them and help drivers get real-time updates on traffic conditions and possible alternate routes. Crime data, when paired with other information such as weather, topographical information, event calendars, and time of year, could provide some useful insights for police to monitor crime more preemptively.

The privacy landscape at this scale is somewhat different from the landscapes at the previous two scales. In a city, people have a reasonable expectation of privacy. However, when a crime is committed and a suspect booked, his or her anonymity is gone. Name, age, and bail amount become part of the public record, often visible via local newspapers. In addition, police units are likely to share their crime data with researchers if they believe it can help them reduce crime in their precincts. This chapter looks at some examples.

I   Traffic Data from the Road and the Crowd

There was a time when most traffic information came from a reporter in a helicopter on the street. But now, thanks to GPS navigation, traffic cameras, and location information from drivers' mobile phones as well as from vehicle sensors designed to collect traffic data, the average driver (and traffic reporter) has access to more detailed information about traffic than ever before. And with the cost of congestion exceeding $100 billion per year in the United States and wasting 34 hours per commuter per year (about 4.5 billion hours collectively), according to the 2011 *Urban Mobility Report*,[2] there's an incentive to find a better route.

Inrix, a company based in Kirkland, Washington, has made it its mission to aggregate a variety of traffic data to make sure navigational devices in people's cars have the most up-to-the-minute information. It is the largest provider of traffic data in the world, with competitors NAVTEQ, TomTom International BV, and Media Mobile sharing the market.[3] Inrix distributes traffic information to such companies as AT&T, BMW, Ford, Garmin, Google, MapQuest, and Sprint.

As of 2010, Inrix, a 2004 Microsoft spinout, had monitored real-time traffic on roughly 260,000 miles of roads in the United States. The types of data Inrix uses to make its travel-time predictions and route suggestions include traffic alerts from police and emergency scanners; historical data compiled by state departments of transportation (DOTs); real-time data from roadway sensors and cameras; crowdsourced data from drivers' mobile phones and GPS units in an ever-increasing fleet of vehicles; event information, including concerts or sports events; and weather and road conditions, as inferred from data collected in cars.

The traditional method of monitoring traffic—essentially a person on the street or in the air—is still used today (e.g., radio traffic reports). Reports from police, emergency scanners, and organizations that operate bridges, tunnels, and highways and from traffic cameras are compiled by companies such as Clear Channel, which sell the information to radio and television stations as well as to Inrix. Data may be available to researchers via purchase or licensing agreements, but the data are typically licensed through device manufacturers (Garmin and TomTom, for example), from which customers must buy a subscription.[4]

The use of public traffic cameras is a quick and easy way to see if a roadway is blocked, and the views of many cameras are available to the public via the Internet.[5] These cameras are used mostly for a qualitative measure of traffic conditions and to spot accidents quickly after they occur, although some companies—the Belgium-based Traficon and the Israeli-based Agent Vi—are producing systems that automatically analyze video data.

Another way to monitor traffic is with sensors built into the road. These so-called embedded loop sensors have been around for decades, and they're still providing useful data. The loop sensors create an electromagnetic field that is disrupted when a car, with its metal undercarriage, passes over it. California had deployed 25,000 loop detectors below its highway system as of 2009 to measure flow, roadway occupancy, and speed. State and federal DOT agencies keep historical databases of traffic data from loop sensors, freely available to the public and sometimes accessible via DOT websites. Inrix incorporates historical data into its traffic prediction algorithms. Historical traffic data can then be used to help plan, for instance, a route through St. Louis at 4:30 p.m. on a Thursday.

A type of sensing technology that Inrix does not use but that has been shown to produce traffic-flow estimates similar to those of Inrix is a set of stationary Bluetooth sensors. The University of Maryland completed a project in 2012 that demonstrated that two Bluetooth sensors permanently placed two miles apart could accurately detect traffic speeds.[6] Roughly one in every 20 cars has an in-use Bluetooth sensor, often for hands-free use of a mobile phone, and this sensor has a unique identification. The first roadside Bluetooth monitor in the pair picks up the mobile ID, and if the ID is detected at the second Bluetooth monitor two miles down the road, the time of travel is calculated.

Although loop sensors, Bluetooth sensors, and traffic cameras are sources of real-time information for Inrix, they do not cover all roads. These types of infrastructure sensors are found mainly on major highways and in major metropolitan areas. Therefore, Inrix has turned to more distributed and granular sources of traffic data: GPS navigation devices and mobile phones within vehicles. Whereas GPS navigation devices are fairly accurate, mobile phones, whose location is most often determined by Wi-Fi and cell tower triangulation, can sometimes miss a mark by 20 feet or more. However, with large numbers of mobile phones, a useful signal can be pulled from the noise. By 2012, Inrix had collected data from roughly 50 million mobile telephones and GPS devices worldwide, mostly in fleet and commercial vehicles. According to the company, most of the crowdsourced data in the United States comes from vehicles using GPS units. In the summer of 2011, Inrix acquired the United Kingdom–based company ITIS, which locates vehicles based on cell tower triangulation. The approach isn't as accurate as GPS and makes up only about 50 percent of localization data from fleets outside the United States, but it helps fill the gaps where GPS devices aren't prevalent.

Inrix also considers events in and around cities and the way similar events have historically affected traffic. Employees at companies that produce events manually aggregate data about the events, and these data are included in traffic predictions and route-suggestion algorithms.

In addition, Inrix has partnered with a number of automotive companies, including Audi, Nissan, and Ford, to provide traffic data for their cars' built-in navigation systems. As of 2012, the company also mines sensor data in cars made by manufacturing partners. Antilock brakes and windshield wiper usage, among other sensors, play a part in determining real-time conditions on the road.

Like Inrix, Google uses mobile phones to help determine traffic conditions.[7] In addition to using information provided by fleet drivers, Google taps location and speed information anonymously from anyone who has enabled GPS on his phone while using Google Maps for mobile. According to the company, the phone sends anonymous data back to Google describing how fast a driver is moving. Combined with the speed of other phones on the road at any given time (Google Maps is installed on more than 200 million mobile devices[8]), the approach provides fairly good live reports. But Google lacks data in some countries, and in the fall of 2011 it partnered with Inrix to fill in those holes.[9]

Google has considered drivers' privacy: speed and location are anonymous and sent to Google servers only when a user has enabled location services on the phone. In addition, when many people report data from the same area, the company combines those data, which makes it hard to distinguish one phone from another. And finally, the start and end points of every trip are permanently deleted so that no one, including employees at Google, has access to that information. Google Maps users' phones that have location service enabled automatically send the data back to the company's servers, but a person can opt out of this transmission by disabling all location services. Although Google offers APIs for some of its mapping data[10]—such as directions, distance, and elevation—its traffic data are not currently available to programmers interested in building their own applications.

In mid-2013, Google acquired the Silicon Valley start-up Waze, which also collected traffic data from people's mobile phones, but only with their explicit consent. In fact, Waze, founded in 2009, relied on its users to flesh out its maps (filling in the name of the blank side road, for example) as well as to report on speed traps, traffic jams, and accidents. In 2012, Waze doubled its user numbers from 10 million to 20 million.[11] The service had become increasingly useful—providing more accurate travel times and offering better alternative routes—as more people from different cities opted in. To increase the number of users and their participation, the company employed "social-gaming" elements that give virtual rewards, points, and badges for using the service.

Mobile phone traffic apps such as those from Google, Waze, and others are attractive to some users because they are inexpensive, provide traffic estimates that are relatively good, and in some cases are fun to use. Although Inrix and TomTom offer mobile apps, their core business is to provide highly accurate traffic analysis for in-car navigation systems. Currently, traffic data from Inrix and crowdsourced-only products are not freely available for download, although some of it may be available via licensing agreements. Since 2008, the University of Maryland has partnered with Inrix and the I-95 Corridor Coalition. Using real-time and historical traffic data collected and aggregated by Inrix for more than 20,000 miles of roads in 10 states through the I-95 corridor (which runs the full length of the east coast, from Florida to Maine), researchers are helping DOTs determine where and how to better allocate transportation resources.[12]

II Data for Predicting Crime

At the core of predicting crime is a solid database of the crimes that have occurred previously. Some of the most relied-upon methods of data collection haven't changed much over the years: police officers still write incident and arrest reports, which are rife with useful information. These incident reports are generated in two main ways. First, a police officer on patrol spots criminal activity. Then she questions the suspects and can make arrests. Or, second, someone calls in a tip or complaint. On reports, police record information such as time, date, location of the crime, the crime code (there are hundreds), more specific information about where the incident occurred (in a convenience store, on the sidewalk, in the street, for example), and the name and contact information of the person who called in with the tip or complaint, if there is such a person.

For decades, the data from incident and arrest reports were processed by a computer and mapped, providing data in a more useful visual-spatial format. These sorts of maps were used for specific cases—to determine geographical boundaries of suspects' activity, for instance. They were also used to provide a sense of the types of crimes in certain neighborhoods and how those crimes might drift or relocate to new areas over time.

More recently, the use of specialized algorithms and real-time crime data is creating frequently updated crime maps that can position police in locations before crimes occur (see chapter 6). In Memphis, Tennessee, police have run a program since 2005 called Blue CRUSH (Criminal Reduction Utilizing Statistical History). Commanders use heat maps of reported crimes to examine current activity levels and shifts in crime levels due to previous changes in police coverage. The maps are updated weekly and used to adjust tactics for the coming week.[13]

In addition to maps that can show geographic relationships between crimes, it's also possible to overlay crime data on maps that include various layers of geographic information, such as topographical data provided by the US Geological Survey.[14] Other helpful measures might include mapping home addresses of criminals and victims and overlaying geographic information, such as roads, school zones, congressional districts, railroads, industries, employment, average income, and other information that is freely available via the US Census Bureau.[15] Also, comparing different sets of crime data—such as drug seizures and thefts of vehicles and the time at which they occurred—could provide insight.

In addition to maps of crime, some researchers and police departments are compiling networked graphs of suspected gang activity. In order to model the relationships between gangs, the Los Angeles Police Department and UCLA used historical data on more than 1,000 gang crimes and suspected gang crimes over 10 years in an area with an estimated 30 gangs. The researchers could identify, 80 percent of the time, the top three most likely gangs to have committed a new crime based on these models.[16]

Researchers at the University of Santa Cruz, using different models developed at UCLA, worked with the Santa Cruz Police Department's data to watch for crime bursts. The observed patterns were similar mathematically to earthquake aftershocks, enabling the department to put officers near locations likely to experience a crime.[17]

III   Video Data to Catch and Possibly Deter Criminals

One data-intensive approach to gathering information about crime is to install video cameras on streets. The US Department of Homeland Security has funded many police departments' cameras in an effort to combat terrorist threats, so the number of public security cameras in the United States has proliferated. In 2009, Homeland Security spent $15 million in seven cities for its Urban Area Security Initiative, a program to address planning, equipment, and training in urban areas to protect against, respond to, and recover from acts of terrorism.[18] In 2010, more than $830 million went to 64 metropolitan areas. In 2011, 31 cities used $662 million dollars of funding under the initiative.[19]

Research is mixed about the effectiveness of these sorts of cameras as crime deterrents. Through analysis of crime cameras in Los Angeles, a 2008 study conducted by the University of Southern California found that there was no statistically significant reduction in violent and property crimes.[20] Similarly, a 2008 study by the University of California at Berkeley saw no reduction in violent crime after San Francisco installed cameras.[21] In 2009, an internal report by the police in London, a city well known for its use of public cameras, found that the cameras rarely helped to catch criminals.[22]

Yet a 2011 report from the Urban Institute examined historic data from 2001 onward from Chicago, Baltimore, and Washington, DC, that revealed more complex results.[23] Chicago had the most extensive camera network of the three; in one area, Humboldt Park, the camera installation correlated with a 12 percent decline in overall crime, whereas a second Chicago area, West Garfield Park, had no drop in crime. Three areas in Baltimore were studied, one with a 25 percent crime reduction, another with a 10 percent reduction, and another with no reduction. In Washington, DC, there was no concurrent drop in crime. The study authors suggest that the best use of the technology is to have trained personnel monitoring live video feeds and be able to move the cameras to get the widest field of view. This recommendation points to the critical nature of camera implementation and maintenance for this sort of data collection.

IV   Public Access

Although the average citizen doesn't have access to most public-camera feeds, he or she does have access to traffic cameras, webcams, and databases of anonymous criminal activity at websites such as crimereports.com and crimemapping.com, which rely on law enforcement to supply data about crime. Both sites let users visualize various crimes on a map. To preserve the privacy of victims of crime, specific addresses are scrubbed, so the locations of incidents are instead presented at the block level. Data aren't available for download, and scraping data from the sites is a violation of the terms of use. Detailed information about sex offenders, including name, age, and address, is available, however, via crimereports.com.

V Legality of Cameras for Traffic and Crime

Traffic cameras, when positioned at a distance from drivers, may seem innocuous, but in 2004 the American Civil Liberties Union complained that police could use these traffic video feeds, monitored live, to make illegal stops, which it claimed violated bans on illegal search and seizure.

In recent years, a new type of street camera has been deployed. Instead of simply watching traffic flow, these cameras snap pictures of drivers' faces and license plates in order to issue tickets for running a red light or speeding. But in 2007 the Minnesota Supreme Court found that cameras that take pictures of drivers at red lights violated a car owner's presumption of innocence. A number of other states, including Wisconsin, West Virginia, South Carolina, New Hampshire, Montana, and Mississippi, prohibit the use of these cameras. But a number of large cities, including Chicago, Baltimore, San Diego, Portland, and Washington, DC, continue to use red-light cameras, often supplied and maintained by private companies, with more than half of the public in these cities approving of their use, according to public-opinion polls.[24]

The use of public cameras—silent video surveillance—for traffic and crime in general has held up relatively well in court. In 1967, the US Supreme Court defined in *Katz v. United States* (389 U.S. 347) the modern search-and-seizure law under the Fourth Amendment. Generally speaking, a person walking on a public sidewalk or standing in a public park can't expect that her activity is private from other passersby or the police. Likewise, a person in a car or on a public road can't expect privacy and may be surveilled. Thus, public videotape of individuals on public roads is allowed.

The legality of such surveillance was further fortified in 1993 with *United States v. Sherman* (990 F.2d 1265), in which the Court of Appeals for the Ninth Circuit held that people videotaped in public view "have no reasonable expectations of privacy, and could not challenge the government's use of videotape at trial as violating the Fourth Amendment."[25]

The legality of camera use in public places suggests that researchers can set up their own cameras for research purposes in public spaces. Indeed, there is precedent for installing cameras on college campuses to do human mobility research.[26] It can be an expensive proposition, however, and many of the researchers who use cameras for projects tap into government-funded and maintained cameras that stream their feeds live online. Currently, most webcam-based research relies on cameras in remote locations for tracking wildlife or environmental features.

VI Conclusion

Although it may be difficult for an individual researcher or entrepreneur to acquire traffic and crime data at the scale of the city, it is possible to partner with companies that collect and compile it, to work with police departments to gain access to historic databases, and to take advantage of freely downloadable government census data. When crime data are used scrupulously, without infringing on an individual's privacy, that use can be a powerful tool to make cities safer.

In addition, researchers may be able to install cameras (that do not record audio) in certain locations to collect urban mobility data on their own, albeit relatively small sample sizes. But even small samples of a given segment of urban life, over time, can provide insights into the rhythm of a city. Police and transportation resources can be better allocated; some researchers have even begun to look at this sort of data to monitor disease outbreaks. Crime and traffic data are an underused resource for building systems that can make cities safer and more livable. In the next chapter, we explore some of the possibilities found in this data.

6 Engineering and Policy: Optimizing Resource Allocation

As technologies enable more extensive analysis of data from the individual scale to the city scale, some people turn to large data sets as a fortune-teller might turn to a crystal ball. Ask the right question, and see the future materialize before your eyes. Even with Big Data and effective analysis, however, the picture of the future can still be murky. Still, the city scale offers an exciting opportunity: build fast-adapting systems for crime and traffic, and your predictions in these areas can be useful.

By analyzing trends in crime data, police departments in Philadelphia, Memphis, and Los Angeles have already developed systems that identify the optimal location of police resources before criminals strike. They've shown that the mere presence of police in these locations can avert serious crimes. When implemented in a respectful way that doesn't threaten law-abiding citizens in high-crime areas, these crime-prediction systems can make communities healthier and safer.

Traffic prediction is another area that shows increasing promise. Companies such as Inrix and Google fuse their multiple data sources to make better estimates of travel times while also providing real-time updates that help people avoid jams or accidents. Using traffic data, researchers from Microsoft are even able to make predictions about future unexpected traffic events. Thanks to Reality Mining, it's now possible to predict unexpected events and surprises.

But forecasting traffic isn't the only use for traffic data. City planners who want to know which roads and intersections are dangerous, which might need upgrades, and how best to evacuate people in an emergency can employ such data. Moreover, traffic data can be used to get a bird's-eye view of general mobility around a city, enabling us to see the temporal flows of a city's inhabitants.

Understanding a city's mobility allows researchers to ask important questions about disease spread: Where did a virus originate? Who should be quarantined? Who needs to be vaccinated? A few researchers are using traffic data, among other mobility indicators, to develop a better sense of how contagions move throughout cities. (A more detailed treatment of tracking disease at the global scale is given in chapter 10.)

This chapter explores the straightforward predictive and more nuanced applications of mining data at the city scale.

I Traffic Prediction and Modeling Surprise

Inrix has developed algorithms that use different data streams—from GPS and Wi-Fi location provided by mobile phones, from GPS location provided by dashboard units, from road sensors and traffic cameras, from historic accounts of traffic, and from event calendars and weather forecasts—to determine the speed of traffic flow for segments of road. The company then uses this information to estimate drive times for entire trips. In addition, it continuously monitors traffic and updates predictions every minute. According to independent research conducted by the

University of Maryland and the I-95 Corridor Coalition, which used stationary Bluetooth sensors to monitor traffic flow on a two-mile segment of road on I-95 (see chapter 5), Inrix's estimates for vehicle speed is accurate within two miles per hour over 24 hours a day and seven days a week.[1]

In 2008, Google offered a feature that allowed users of web-based Google Maps to estimate driving time for a future trip.[2] If a person wanted to see what the drive time to a doctor's appointment would be, incorporating the time and day of the appointment, she could use this feature. It was quickly abandoned, however, and hasn't been reissued on the Web. It should be noted that Google Maps on iPhone and Android phones offers drive-time estimates, but not a tool to estimate driving time for a future trip.

As good as some traffic predictions systems are, they still fail when the unexpected happens. However, although it may seem impossible to predict a surprise such as an overturned egg truck or an unexpectedly clear road, researchers at Microsoft have found a way to make some reasonable estimates for when a surprise might strike. Called "surprise modeling," the approach could improve traffic estimates as well as other areas in which prediction might play a role: health care, military strategy, and financial markets, to name a few.

Surprise modeling grew out of a Microsoft software project called SmartPhlow started in 2003 by Eric Horvitz and colleagues. The software showed traffic flow on highways, but it also alerted users to surprises, such as when a road unexpectedly cleared or when a clear road suddenly jammed. Using data from several years of Seattle traffic and relating the data to accidents, weather, holiday, and events, the researchers divided the day into 15-minute segments and computed the probability distribution of traffic for each situation. They paid close attention to anomalous traffic, where the data deviated significantly from the averaged model. Each of these surprises was noted, as were events up to 30 minutes prior that might have led up to the deviation. The researchers then examined the conditions prior to the surprises to see if there were a pattern. The result was a system that, at a false-positive rate of 5 percent, predicted 50 percent of the surprises on the road that a driver would later encounter.[3]

II   Road Resources: Infrastructure Planning, Emergency Response, Evacuations

Interstate 95 is the north–south highway that runs from Maine through Florida. Since 2008, the I-95 Corridor Coalition—a partnership of transportation agencies; public-safety, port, and transit organizations in the eastern seaboard states; the University of Maryland; and Inrix—has been conducting research to find ways to turn the billions of traffic data points into information that can be used to improve the transportation network. The initiative, Vehicle Probe Project (VPP), relies on crowdsourced data, such as the data from GPS units in cars, and extends to at least 2014.

As well as providing more accurate information to travelers via websites such as I95travelinfo.net and 511 phone and web services, the project aims to help city-planning organizations make better decisions. Planners in Washington, DC, and Philadelphia, for instance, are using VPP data to determine highway network performance. It's a first step for planning highway improvements that can limit congestion and accommodate changes in overall travel patterns.

The flood of data from the VPP has also enabled emergency response teams to get to accidents more quickly. In New Jersey, for instance, traffic operations staff identified through VPP a serious accident on a stretch of Interstate 80 during a surprise snowstorm in October 2008 that wouldn't have been seen by a camera-based system,[4] allowing them to dispatch emergency personnel faster.

Traffic data can also be used to help county and state governments evacuate people more effectively in disasters. Florida, in the path of multiple hurricanes a year, is a good example of a state that is especially invested in the smooth flow of traffic during evacuations, which are coordinated primarily at the county level, with state officials coordinating on a larger scale.

With access to real-time traffic data during evacuations, Florida state officials can see the directions citizens are driving and inform neighboring counties and states so that resources for evacuees can be available. In addition, "contraflow" measures can be enacted on particularly congested evacuation routes, which direct evacuees to alternate evacuation routes or ad hoc emergency shelters.[5]

III Looking at Traffic to Track Germs

One of the great benefits of large amounts of traffic data is the ability to get a bird's-eye view of the way people move in a city. Epidemiologists in particular are finding value in traffic data. Researchers who track outbreaks of diseases now use traffic information to see how people—and the contagions they may or may not carry—move throughout a city.

A measure of a city's mobility can be factored into models of disease spread that estimate where an outbreak started, where it's spreading to, and how quickly it's moving. This information can be used for issuing reasonable quarantine and vaccination measures and for putting resources—such as hospital staff—in the right places at the right times.

A number of researchers, including Alessandro Vespignani and Dirk Brockman, use transportation data to model mobility in disease networks at various scales. Vespignani and his colleagues have found differences in the commuting flows of traffic at the city scale compared to those of airline traffic. Commuting flows are an order of magnitude more intense than airline traffic, which means there are more and more varied interactions and connections between people at the city scale. This finding highlights the importance of understanding the nuances of mobility data at various scales. Vespignani and his colleagues suggest that models developed at the city scale should be included in global disease networks to make the overall model more accurate as well as to offer granularity.[6]

IV Crime Stats for Predictive Policing

Police departments as a matter of course collect data about crime: incident reports that entail the who, what, when, where, and how of suspected illegal activity. Over the past decade or so, much of this crime data has gone digital, which has provided the opportunity to mine it for patterns that help departments make better decisions about where to send squad cars on Friday night and the number of officers to assign to cover major events such as a Sunday football game.

New York City is an example of a municipality well known for its computerized crime system, Compstat, which it began using in 1994. Compstat, now used in cities across the United States, keeps track of long-term trends in reported illegal activity. The 2011 book *The City That Became Safe* by Franklin E. Zimring suggests that it's possible Compstat influenced the city's drop in crime over the past decades. With Compstat, departments were able to place more police in the areas where crime tended to happen.[7]

In the past decade, a handful of police departments have taken the spirit of Compstat to heart but added a twist. Whereas Compstat data have historically been used in weekly strategy meetings and rely on humans to recognize patterns in them, a number of new crime-tracking systems are updated daily, using algorithms to predict future crime in near real time.[8]

Much of the basis of this real-time crime tracking comes from work published in 2004 by researchers at Carnegie Mellon University in collaboration with the Pittsburgh Police Department. Jacqueline Cohen, Wilpen Gorr, and Andreas Olligsch-laeger combed through 1.3 million police records for 16 crime types—from larceny to murder—in Pittsburgh for January 1991 to December 1998. The goal was to provide month-ahead forecasts for crime in the city, broken down into a grid system of 104 square cells that encompassed about 100 blocks per cell.

The researchers found that they could find the leading indicators (other crimes) for serious crimes and determine how large an effect these indicators had. With this information, they developed a forecast model that helped police decide where to send officers, whose presence presumably prevented crime increases, and where to withdraw if there were a low risk of crime at that time. The methods used to predict incidents relied on correlations between crimes. The researchers concluded that their methods of correlating crimes were significantly better than a standard extrapolation method that simply looks at the trend in a single type of crime.[9]

Although criminal activity might have dropped in Pittsburgh and New York, it was up in Santa Cruz. From 2000 to 2011, the number of incidents rose, but unfortunately due to state and city budget cuts the number of police officers is down. In 2011, in an effort to help police patrol more effectively, the Santa Cruz Police Department partnered with researchers George Tita, George Mohler, Martin Short, and Jeff Brantingham to develop and test a workable crime-prediction system. The researchers broke the city into a grid of 500 feet by 500 feet and plotted eight years of Santa Cruz incident reports.[10] Unlike Compstat, their system took on new data daily. It also employed computer models traditionally used to predict earthquake aftershocks that apply well to predicting crime, and police were given daily updates about new crime hot spots. Anecdotally, the system appears to be reducing crime somewhat. Final analysis wasn't available at the time of writing (2013), however.

Like Santa Cruz, Memphis was suffering from rising crime in the 2000s. But pay freezes and shrinking budgets meant that the solution wouldn't come just by hiring more police for broader coverage. So in 2005 the Memphis Police Department developed Blue CRUSH (Criminal Reduction Utilizing Statistical History) with IBM,[11] a system mentioned in chapter 5. Using police reports that go back nearly a decade as well as data updated in real time by hand-held digital devices used by police in the field, the system looks for correlations between crime, location, and other variables such as abandoned housing. In addition to informing police as to where to patrol, it's also useful for employing security cameras more effectively—knowing where to position them and when to monitor them. With the use of Blue CRUSH, Memphis has seen a 30 percent reduction in serious crime overall and a 15 percent reduction in violent crime.

Clearly, there are many different approaches and models for crime data analysis, dictated by the types of questions police departments want to ask and the resources they have to allocate. In addition to reducing crime, these systems offer city governments, such as those of Santa Cruz and Memphis, ways to allocate police resources more effectively, especially in times when budgets are tight.

V Conclusion

Both traffic and crime data are fertile ground for deploying models for prediction. More efficient evacuations, emergency responses, and contagion tracking are just some of the uses for traffic data. Surprise modeling, first developed for predicting unexpected traffic events, has applications in other areas as well, including crime.

An important consideration when developing crime-prediction systems, in particular, is to consider the manner in which those systems are implemented and how they might affect communities that suffer from high crime. It's not new for police to patrol neighborhoods or blocks that could harbor crime, driving or walking routes according to their hunches and conventional wisdom. But it is new to station police at a specific place to wait for trouble. If executed without proper training and oversight, such a system could lead to profiling of types of people, harassment of innocent citizens, and unnecessary arrests. The power and potential of crime-prediction systems is impressive, and such systems will continue to gain popularity. As they do, it's crucial to keep in mind that implementing them matters. It might be helpful to involve community leaders in discussions of the new technology before it's rolled out. Not only can concerns be heard and trust built, but further insights from people on the ground would add to the veracity of crime data. It's a smart way to get a reality check about the true state of illegal activity and to develop a respectful approach that would be critical to maintaining the overall success of such programs.

IV   The Nation (1 Million to 100 Million People)

7 Taking the Pulse of a Nation: Census, Mobile Phones, and Internet Giants

As Reality Mining scales up, national governments, large companies, and international organizations begin to play a crucial role in the collection, compilation, and dissemination of data. At this national scale, researchers and entrepreneurs can gain access to a wide range of data sources, including national censuses; call records; major Internet companies such as Google, Facebook, and Twitter; and, to a limited extent, banks. Of course, some of these data are more readily available than others.

Census data are by far the easiest to acquire. Many nations make their census findings public via websites from which data can be downloaded and visualized for further analysis. In addition, the World Bank conducts international surveys and compiles census data from all participating nations—a sort of one-stop shop for information on its member countries. These data are publicly accessible: they can be downloaded and independently sorted and analyzed. Importantly, the World Bank offers an open API that allows programmers to integrate various data into software applications. Using World Bank data, Google has integrated a simple visualization tool into its search results; a search query on the population of Botswana will pull up the number, the dated World Bank source, and a graph showing population change over decades.

Another emerging source of data, especially useful for understanding the mobility of people within a country or region, is call data records or call detail records (CDRs). Unlike census and World Bank data, however, CDRs are much more difficult for the average entrepreneur or researcher to access.

As a data set, a CDR contains a log of communication (calls and text messages) and transactional events, including information about the caller or sender and the recipient as well as the time, location, and, in the case of calls, duration. Historically, CDRs have been used exclusively for billing purposes, but starting in 2005 researchers at network service providers and universities began to recognize the value of such data, especially for modeling human mobility. A few researchers and entrepreneurs have agreements to use some mobile carrier data with various limitations. Some mobile carriers are willing to share anonymized CDRs as long as legal agreements detail that no proprietary and personal information will ever be made public. An additional stipulation of such agreements might be that researchers demonstrate to the operators the value of their proposed analysis—for example, the possible development of predictive models of "churn," referring to subscription termination and product adoption.

The national scale is also where we first address the importance of the major Internet data collectors Google, Facebook, and Twitter. These companies have profound effects on the individuals, communities, and governments who use them, but their power as tools of mass data collection becomes apparent at this scale. The obvious application of data collected by Internet companies is targeted advertising. But the data provide other untapped opportunities, including the chance for targeted market-research surveys and disease tracking (see chapter 10).

Twitter, designed to make most user input publicly available in real time, can be used to track national sentiment as well as the possible allocation of resources during national disasters or other times of crises.

Some of the applications for Google, Facebook, and Twitter are discussed in detail in chapter 8, and some are highlighted in chapter 10 because the effect of these international companies are also felt on a global scale. Both part IV and part V of this book, in fact, address a number of types of data—CDRs, data sets owned by Internet companies, bank data, and more—that can be collected at both the national scale and the international scale and then used for applications at both levels. This chapter takes a first look at some of the data collected at the national scale and how those data might be accessed. We also look at questions of privacy, specifically in the use of anonymized CDRs. Even if identifying information is stripped from the logs, it is possible to reconstruct a person's identity by cross-referencing easily accessed public information such as census data. We describe one promising approach, currently in development, that could give researchers and entrepreneurs access to CDRs while still allowing them to maintain individual anonymity.

I Census and Survey: Public Records of the People

Today, most countries conduct a census, and many of them make the data publicly available on the Web. The US government, for instance, makes resources available through American Fact Finder.[1] A person can search on the site by topic (such as age and income); geography (such as state and county); race, ethnicity, or tribe; and industry, product, or commodity name. In addition to census data, a person can download data from other surveys, including the Economic Census, taken every five years, and the Population Estimates Program, which publishes up-to-date population estimates for towns, cities, countries, and states.[2]

In 2009, the US government launched an online data repository called data.gov that provides more than 445,000 raw and geospatial data sets across governmental agencies, encompassing such categories as business, arts, recreation and travel, elections, foreign aid, transportation, welfare, and others.[3] Examples of these data sets include "Personnel Trends by Gender/Race," "Active Mines and Mineral Plants in the U.S.," "Quarterly Report on Bank Derivatives Activity," and "Wild Horse and Burro Population Count." The data can be downloaded in XML, Text/CSV, KML/KMZ, Feeds, XLS, and ESRI Shapefile formats, and several already interactive data sets have their own APIs so programmers can integrate maps and charts into web applications.[4]

One of the richest collections of nation-scale public data comes from the World Bank.[5] This international organization offers a data catalog that includes databases, preformatted tables, reports, and other resources.[6] In sum, more than 7,000 indicators—from percentage of agricultural land to literacy rate—are available for download from the site. In addition, the site allows a person to browse data by more than 200 countries and economies, by topics such as health or climate change, and by indicators such as gross domestic product or gasoline prices.

The Development Data Group[7] at the World Bank coordinates the data collection and statistical analysis and maintains a number of the databases used by the World Bank to prepare assistance strategies, assess poverty, and perform research. A large portion of the data comes from the 187 member countries,[8] working with the World Bank and its partners[9] to improve the capacity, efficiency, and effectiveness of national statistics systems.[10]

The World Bank claims to operate with the highest professional data standards possible, using two main frameworks to assess statistics systems: the General Data Dissemination System and the Data Quality Assessment Framework, both jointly developed with the International Monetary Fund.[11] The organization acknowledges, however, that there are inconsistencies in data sets due to various participating nations' timing and reporting practices: all data are collected by traditional survey, which results in relatively sparse data sets. Therefore, the World Bank recommends combining data sets with caution. For its part, the organization provides its methods of data aggregation of economic data, growth-rate calculations, and conversion factors that are affected by exchange rate to make cross-data-set comparisons as accurate as possible.[12]

In addition to searching data sets on the World Bank site and downloading tables, users can also access the data via three different APIs: one for indicators, one for projects (data on World Bank operations), and one for World Bank financial data.[13] The APIs allow for programmatic access to more than 3,000 indicators via queries within adjustable parameters. The World Bank provides API access to many data series from 50 years ago and includes data from closed projects, active projects, and projects in progress.

Google incorporates World Bank data into a visualization and comparison tool called Google Public Data Explorer, which allows people to slice and dice data from World Bank records as well as from 60 other various public data sets.[14] In order to download the data to perform more sophisticated analysis, however, a person must visit individual websites for the actual data sets.

II Call Data Records: Beyond Caller ID

In order to bill customers and understand call loads on their networks, mobile phone network service providers keep records of their customers' phone use. Among other metrics, these CDRs contain the time and general location where a call or text was made (via cell tower ID) and the recipient of the call. CDRs are a particularly attractive source of location information for mobility research because of the current prevalence of mobile phones. In addition, CDRs provide location information at little cost compared to labor-intensive surveys that sample only a small subset of a population.

In recent years, researchers at network service providers, universities, and start-ups have begun to see how this sort of data might determine models of human mobility and social networks. (Chapter 8 explores specific applications of CDR-based models.) Accessing such CDRs, however, poses a major challenge for most researchers and entrepreneurs. Due to privacy concerns and proprietary rules, mobile carriers do not make their data broadly available to the public. Therefore, the researchers who do have access have it because they are able to provide specific analysis techniques, to improve models, or to offer something else of value to mobile carriers, such as determining the likelihood that a customer will cancel his mobile service. If you're a researcher or entrepreneur who would like CDRs for a purpose that isn't directly applicable to a mobile phone company's needs, you may need to spend some of your research time doing work that directly aids the operator.

Mobile carriers' hesitation in sharing these data comes in part from potential public-relations issues about privacy concerns. And with good reason. Since 2005, when the *New York Times* brought to light a program sanctioned by the US government to mine CDRs from AT&T for the sake of national security, and in recent years with revelations of the National Security Agency's PRISM data-mining program, the sensitivity of these records has been in the public eye. Lawsuits have followed, some of which have found the government guilty of unlawful surveillance, but others have been overturned on technicalities.[15]

Although the warrantless government search of specific customers' CDRs is different from researchers modeling a population's aggregate behavior with CDRs, mobile operators are still careful about making the data broadly available. Even when large data sets are anonymized and the customer-identifying information such as the handset identifier and phone number are stripped, it's still possible to reconstruct an individual's identity. Past studies have shown that with just a few identifiers, such as gender, birthdate, and zip code, a person can be identified, even if more sensitive information such as name, address, and social security number is not available. Using these three identifiers crossed with census data, 63 percent to 87 percent of the US population (depending on the census year) can be uniquely identified.[16]

In one example of deanonymizing a CDR, researchers from Sprint used a data set of 30 billion calls made by 25 million mobile users across all 50 states in the United States. The researchers inferred the top locations of each user and correlated it with publicly available census data. The researchers then concluded that almost all users could be identified given enough time to determine top locations such as "home" and "work" based on cell phone location. They suggest that in order to maintain anonymity, at a minimum, the data must be coarse in time and in space, meaning that it is collected in a day rather than during a month and over geographic regions larger than the range of a single cellular tower.[17]

Researchers at AT&T are trying to make available to the masses the sort of information that makes CDRs so valuable, but also to do so while maintaining privacy. A project by Sibren Isaacman at Princeton, Ramón Cáceres at AT&T, and their colleagues, called WHERE ("Work and Home Extracted Regions"), aims to develop a synthetic model of mobile users for a particular city. By using AT&T records of spatial input and temporal probability distributions derived directly from empirical data, WHERE creates data for synthetic mobile phone customers. Synthetic CDRs have been created for New York and Los Angeles metropolitan areas and validated against billions of anonymous locations samples from hundreds of thousands of phones in those cities. The main benefit of these synthetic CDRs is that they maintain the privacy of individuals because no data from real individuals are used. In addition, the researchers claim that WHERE is more accurate than other approaches to mobile phone data modeling. (In one example, the daily range of travel statistics falls within one mile of their true values.) Still very much in the research phase, this sort of project could allow broader access to the type of data contained in CDRs.[18]

III Google, Facebook, Twitter

No introduction is needed for these three Internet giants, but it is important to mention some particulars of the data each collects and the differences in general access between them. Google's data collection has expanded drastically since its early days, when it simply monitored its users' search terms. Because it now owns and operates a number of different types of web services, including Gmail, the Google+ social network, YouTube, and the Chrome web browser, it has access to more data about individual users than ever before. If a feature on Chrome called "Instant" is enabled, the company keeps a log of searches and URLs entered into the browser bar. In addition, for advertising purposes, Google logs YouTube videos watched, activity on Google+, and the text of emails sent through Gmail.[19]

Although the average person can't mine the totality of Google's search terms and customer data, there are some ways to take a biopsy of sorts. By joining AdSense, for instance, one can home in on certain words or phrases that might appear in emails sent and received through Gmail. By outbidding the competition for an ad using those words or phrases, a person can then do an Internet provider lookup to see the location and number of people who receive the ads in Gmail. In this way, a person can find the prevalence of a specific emailed word, potentially pointing to a trend or sentiment across countries.

Similar to Google, Facebook offers an advertising network. When you create an ad, you choose the key words you want associated with it. The ad will then appear on people's profiles that include those words. It's possible to target broad demographics or home in on specific information available on a person's profile: location (city, state, province, or country), demographics (age range, gender, language, relationship status), likes and interests, education, and work.[20] Although the company doesn't make identifying information of the Facebook users who view the ad available to the person who creates a Facebook ad, the advertiser will be given metrics for the number of profiles matching the ad's criteria.

Both AdSense and Facebook ads come in two forms: cost per click (CPC) ads and cost per thousand impressions (CPM) ads. Both can be purchased by placing a bid on the company's site. The companies provide metrics on ads that are useful to people trying to sell particular products or services. These metrics include the number of times the ad is clicked (clicks), the number of times the ad is shown to a user regardless of clicks (impressions), the number of clicks the ad receives divided by the number of times the ad is shown (click-through rate), and the amount being paid for each click on the ad (cost per click). Both companies also provide general statistics such as the number of emails or profiles your ad appears in. It's this information that can be mined to determine overall sentiment toward a product across demographics.

Facebook also offers an API that allows programmers to build applications that plug into Facebook users' profiles.[21] From these applications, a programmer can get access to as much information as a Facebook customer allows in his or her privacy settings, including phone numbers, contact lists, status updates, and any other identifying information.

Some of the most popular Facebook applications, such as those made by the social-gaming company Zynga,[22] not only contain personal identifying information but also collect the habits and behavior of people who play the games. Hundreds of apps have audiences of millions of users,[23] thanks largely to their approach in offering a specific function that has a viral component or particularly satisfying payoff. Simply designing an app to collect information isn't good enough. It must also become popular enough to provide a large enough sample size to be useful. With applications, however, it is difficult to scale adoption rates to collect a significant sample of user data.

Twitter differs significantly from Google and Facebook in that most of the users' data are publicly available. Twitter offers an

API called "Twitter fire hose" that provides access to the constant stream of data that can be used to mine for the sentiment of a nation, thanks to the inclusion of location data with some tweets. Chapter 12 looks more extensively at applications specific to Twitter analyses and how they can be used to understand trends at the national scale. The biggest challenge with Twitter data, however, is to distinguish the signal from noise. Tweets contain highly unstructured information—fragments of conversations, links, hashtags, and abbreviations—that can be a challenge to parse.

IV Banking Transactions

Banking transactions are another source of information at the national scale, but it should be noted that it is nearly impossible to access data from commercial transactions. Banks tend to use data analytics to watch for fraud or to predict when someone might switch banks or to adjust interest rates depending on spending habits or risk. For researchers and entrepreneurs, customer-spending data have the potential to provide powerful insights into mobility and decision making. Because location is coupled with a specific action—the purchasing of goods—researchers can gain access to a fine-grained picture of a person's economic behavior, providing insights that even a CDR cannot.

In 2008, Bank of America partnered with MIT to let researchers investigate its database of 80 million customer transactions. Katherine Krumme focused on a subsample of 10,000 customers between 2006 and 2009, with metrics including transaction data; amount; whether a check, debit, or credit card was used; merchant; merchant category code; and whether the transaction took place on- or offline. The transactions included in the study totaled $30–35 billion a month.[24]

This isn't the sort of data that falls into the lab of a curious researcher everyday. But there are some signs that well-targeted start-ups, such as Tresata in North Carolina, might be able to partner with big banks by providing data analytics platforms that focus exclusively on the structured and unstructured data particular to the financial industry.[25]

Another financial company, Mint,[26] owned by Intuit, has slipped a siphon into the financial transaction stream by offering a consumer product that links directly to customers to track spending online. With more than 4 million users, Mint provides visualizations of the way a person spends money and offers deals on products such as credit cards, but it also owns direct access to the transactions of its millions of customers. With this information, the company advertises products specifically targeted to an individual's spending patterns. With the data of more than 4 million customers, the company might also provide some aggregate insight into the health of the economy and possibly make predictions on larger scales than simply the sort of credit card a customer might be interested in using.

V Conclusion

Although there are clearly some inherent challenges in accessing data beyond what is publicly available via the censuses, there seem to be opportunities as well. Call data records, despite being off limits to most, could be shared in a controlled way as more and more mobile carriers are seeing the value in partnering with start-ups that can provide insight to the carriers' records, as some universities have done already. Synthetic data sets such as WHERE could also become an important tool if they can be applied more broadly, beyond city limits.

Google and Facebook provide troves of data for those interested in building and paying for ads that target people across demographics and regions who use particular search terms and who have particular interests. It's a relatively untapped source of highly specific data across demographics and regions. Likewise, though more challenging to parse, Twitter already offers much more readily available information that can provide insights.

Big bank data might be the most difficult to access at this point; however, the financial industry might find that the mobile operator model could work for it as well if it should partner with researchers and start-ups that offer some type of value. Financial institutions might find that some Reality-Mining practitioners can also provide synthetic financial data sets that are useful. Although big financial data aren't quite ready yet to be mined for broad-reaching applications, this is certainly a space to keep an eye on. Likewise, as more applications of data at this scale arise, data guardians could start to open up access. The next chapter details some possible applications of this sort of data.

8 Engineering and Policy: Addressing National Sentiment, Economic Deficits, and Disasters

National repositories of data are crucial for understanding how to allocate resources and design policy. But finding the best way to make sense of those data has always been the crucial question. Census, data.gov, and World Bank data all provide important but often static insights into nation-scale populations. These sources provide a snapshot in time and place, constrained by the logistics of traditional data-collection techniques. Through data visualization, such as timelines, maps, and graphs, policymakers and nongovernmental organizations can see the different ways these massive, dynamic data can be sliced, diced, and cross-correlated. The results can lead to more and better services for the poor and hungry, an understanding of voter behavior, and opportunities for early investment in industries that might otherwise remain hidden.

Visualizations to help uncover these potential applications come in many forms. Google offers a tool called Google Public Data Explorer that uses World Bank information as well as other data sets to let people compare various statistics over time. Data .gov links to a number of US government and nongovernment data visualizations, often overlaying the data on maps.

The data visualization team Development Seed uses World Bank data, among other data sets, to create interactive maps. Its spin-off project, Mapbox, allows others to easily and quickly make interactive maps from open data. Development Seed's visualizations usually have specific goals in mind, such as "identifying key problems, strategizing opportunities, building solutions, and designing communications."[1] For instance, one such visualization focused on hunger trends in the Horn of Africa and fair elections in Afghanistan.

At the national scale, one of the major differentiators between data sets is the speed at which they are refreshed. Census and World Bank data refreshes slowly. Mobile phone data refreshment, however, is fast. CDRs (see chapter 7) can provide mobility information in near real time. Combining this new mobility information with historic CDRs from mobile phones, engineers can start to get a picture of mobility and movement networks. With this information, it is possible, for instance, to correlate the population flows of slums to the price of food staples. Ultimately, the models could help predict population influxes and allocate the right resources in the right location at the right time.

In addition to exploring census and CDR data synthesis, this chapter also investigates an approach to using Google and Facebook ad networks to mine real-time sentiment across demographics at the national scale. In some ways, it's like creating a personal poll—ask a specific question by designating search terms or profile key words that call up your ad, then simply monitor the metrics. In this manner, a person can create a series of single-variable polls to get a sense of how a specific population or demographic is feeling. For instance, one might keep track of people who "like" certain political candidates on their Facebook profiles in the months prior to an election.

In addition, this chapter looks at the United Nations Global Pulse project that mines tweets in Indonesia, Twitter's fourth-largest market, to better understand the stressors that the population experiences. Using text analysis, the project is able to illustrate the sentiment surrounding fuel, food, debt, and other factors that indicate stress and thus to predict crisis.

Finally, we discuss applications in the burgeoning area of financial data analysis. Difficult-to-access financial data sets, in particular those collected and analyzed in real time, can provide an instant view of a country's economic health and well-being.

I Demographic Snapshots

When creating public policy for a nation, it's crucial to have quantitative data on the needs, resources, and demographic makeup of various regions.

But because the World Bank has more than 7,000 indicators, from education levels to military expenditure, provided by more than 200 countries, it might be difficult to identify the most important information.[2] To help make sense of the data sets, the World Bank provides an API[3] that allows other organizations and even independent programmers to plug into the data sources. Google Public Data Explorer is an easily accessed, easy-to-use example.[4] By combining World Bank data with 60 other publicly available data sets, this interactive tool allows people to see trends over time and to compare different countries and different statistics and to answer questions such as "Which countries' literacy rates are improving?" "How does this correlate to GDP changes?"

The approach taken by Development Seed, a visualization organization based in Washington, DC, differs from Google's approach in that it creates stylized, visually compelling maps and charts that focus on specific issues. In addition, the programmers and designers at Development Seed work closely with partner organizations to find the best ways to visually answer questions and ultimately affect policy. The organization's recent offering, Mapbox, is an attempt to make mapping various open data sets easier and faster for the public.

One powerful example of a Development Seed Mapbox project maps the effect of the 2011 famine in the Horn of Africa—a combination of drought, conflict, and rising food prices—that affected 13 million people. Using data from the US Agency of International Development and the United Nations Office for the Coordination of Humanitarian Affairs, the organization created maps of current and projected famine levels and drought conditions. These maps could be modified so that others could add layers of information on top of those already there. But the main purpose was to spread the word about the famine and enlist people to donate money to the World Food Programme toward this specific need.[5]

Journalists as well as policymakers are also interested in historic data and trends over time that illustrate improvements, lack of improvements, and general changes in population, economics, political affiliation, and religion, among other metrics. Development Seed has worked with National Public Radio to show the changes in population throughout the United States, with a focus on increases in the Hispanic population and which states and counties they make their home.[6] This is the sort of data that's important when reporting on political, social, or economic events in order to provide perspective and context for a story.

Another Development Seed project is the interactive-map-based Opportunity Index for the United States, which illustrates how states and counties perform across various indicators, including unemployment rate, household income, high-speed Internet subscriptions, education levels, volunteerism, and access to healthy food.[7] These indicators could ultimately be used to help people relocate for work and to spur government or corporate improvement programs in various sectors.

Development Seed has also developed a climate-change map with projected temperature and precipitation changes across the globe. When coupled with World Bank data, which illustrates the types of industries and the income of the people of specific regions, this map becomes a powerful tool to predict climate-change-related economic trouble, including natural disasters such as floods and crop failure.[8]

Maps melded with other data sources related to the effects of climate change could be one of the more powerful tools used today by activists, scientists, and politicians looking to mitigate the expensive consequences of climate change. These data can also be of use to investors who see business opportunities in places where climate change will have large effects. Rising sea levels could be good news, for instance, for construction companies that build levies and other structures to protect against flood. In general, however, these maps and data sets can be used to build compelling cases, potentially across national borders, for the need to decrease greenhouse gas emissions and develop technologies with less impact on the climate.

II Mobility Matters

Although census, World Bank, and other government data sets are important for illustrating slow-moving social and economic trends, they lack granularity and timeliness. CDRs can fill in these gaps. Because CDRs provide an approximation of mobility and a social network throughout a region and country, they can be used to model human behavior, to spot changes in behavior quickly, and to predict future changes in behavior. Fundamental research using CDRs has been able to identify patterns in the way people form connections with others—real-life social-networking ties—and the way they travel. Ultimately, CDR analysis can be applied to specific scenarios. They can, for instance, help governments better understand the dynamics of impermanent settlements such as slums in order to allocate resources better and to predict the repercussions of natural disasters such as earthquakes on those settlements.

Two influential pieces of early work on CDR are Albert-László Barabási and his colleagues' widely cited *Nature* papers from 2007[9] and 2008.[10] These papers illustrated the potential of CDRs as a detailed proxy for the dynamics of human social networks and physical mobility.

The 2007 work on the evolution of social networks used anonymous call records of more than 4 billion users from an undisclosed service provider. With these data, the researchers determined different dynamics of small groups (circles of friends, families, and professional cliques) and large groups (overlapping communities such as schools, institutions, and companies) over time. Small groups were more stable if fewer members of the group were replaced during a given period of time. Large groups, conversely, were more stable when experiencing fluctuations in size and composition.[11]

The 2008 work focused on the mobility dynamics of 100,000 anonymous mobile phone users. Previously, human mobility predictions using Levy flight and random walk models effectively underpredicted the amount of an individual's spatial and temporal regularity.[12] Location data gleaned from CDRs showed that despite differences between various people's past travel patterns, an individual tends to follow simple and reproducible patterns of movement.[13] In a 2010 paper in *Science*, Barabási and his colleagues showed that even with a diverse mix of volume and destinations of travel, most people's mobility can be predicted about 93 percent of the time. And even travelers with the most inconsistent patterns can be predicted to at least 80 percent of the time using models derived from CDR data.[14]

The work by Barabási and his colleagues points to the enormous potential of CDR data sets. When applied to real-life problems, CDRs can illuminate a social, environmental, or economic situation that would otherwise be difficult to probe.

Around the world, more than 1 billion people live in 200,000 slums, heavily populated areas marked by poverty, dirt, and rundown and often improvised housing, as well as in other informal human settlements. Hundreds of millions of these people use mobile phones. Therefore, it's possible to get a dynamic picture of the daily, monthly, and yearly movement patterns of the people who live in such slums. These models of mobility can help confirm and refine existing theories on slum dynamics. For instance, how do the population and mobility of people in slums affect nearby cities? What makes the population of a slum ebb or flow? With answers to these questions, various organizations could develop ways to support people or design effective incentives to help people find more permanent residences.

Amy Wesolowski and Nathan Eagle used mobile phone records to investigate one of the largest slums in the world, Kibera, located southwest of Nairobi's city center. The researchers were able to find migration patterns in and out of Kibera, which allowed them to infer places of work and tribal affiliations. One striking finding was residents' high mobility rates. Almost half of the residents changed the location where they spent the night at least once each month. When trying to infer new places of residence, tribal affiliations, and work regions, the researchers found little overlap from month to month. They called the regions where many people go to spend the day, presumably for work, "economic springboards" and tracked these locations over time.[15]

The researchers suggest that by identifying patterns in the locations of these economic opportunities, they would be able to build predictive models for slum dynamics that, for example, might estimate the location of a new slum, how a slum might grow, and how it might affect the growth of a surrounding urban area. Local municipalities have precious few resources to allocate to ensure slum inhabitants' well-being. Building a better understanding of how the slum will change over time makes it possible to identify the optimal locations for fixed infrastructure investment—such as where to install the next clean water pipe or latrine.

In addition to providing mobility models for long-term challenges such as slums, CDRs can be mined for clues for the best way to respond to acute disasters such as earthquakes. Eagle and his colleagues examined the changes in call logs as a result of an earthquake in February 2008 in the region of Lac Kivu in the Democratic Republic of the Congo. Changes in CDRs from a baseline activity were used to detect the time of the quake and the location of the epicenter and to find regions where anomalous call behavior persisted, which could indicate possible needs for assistance.[16] The ability to use CDRs for these purposes suggests that predictive analysis of natural disasters might be performed within existing telecommunications infrastructure, which could lead to proactive planning to mitigate famine and the spread of disease.

In 2012 in sub-Saharan Africa, malaria killed more than 1 million children under the age of five. One of the major reasons governments and health organizations haven't been successful at containing the disease is a limited understanding of how people, the malaria host, move around in underserved, understudied communities in the region. In an unprecedented data-sharing collaboration involving the Kenyan Ministry of Health, local mobile phone service operators, and several of the world's foremost malaria experts, Eagle and his collaborators gained conclusive evidence that mobile phone data are the most accurate way to quantify the spread of the malaria parasites across regional host populations.[17]

It is now possible to measure the rate, scale, and direction of movement of people on a national level. Combined with well-informed parasite-risk maps, mobile data have allowed researchers for the first time to identify the risk a given location incurs of importing malaria—essentially locating the malaria hot spot. The discovery of malaria hot spots is changing the way malaria control resources are being allocated across Kenya. Officials are now deploying massive amounts of malaria eradication resources diverted from traditional strategies to new ones that incorporate a data-driven insight into people's actual mobility patterns. The researchers' method of combining mobile data with infectious disease and malaria expertise has established a successful new approach for tracking and predicting disease spread and for allocating resources in a smart and efficient manner.

III   Roll Your Own Polling App

When most people want to advertise through Google and Facebook, they're interested in directing business to their company. But in addition to driving sales, Google and Facebook ads have the potential to open a window onto enormous stores of data that, in effect, could give a real-time snapshot of sentiment and opinions on the Web. Both Google AdSense and Facebook Ads provide metrics on the reach of a given advertisement. And because these ads are linked by chosen key words with Google and by demographics and interests with Facebook, a person who produces a series of ads or campaigns can extract metrics on the (unidentified) people who received the ads.

Here's the scenario: You create an AdSense campaign based around key words such as *flu* and *feeling sick*. You then watch over time how your metrics for these key words, which may be searched or appear in emails through Gmail, change. For instance, there may be a gradual increase in the number of people who see these ads in the fall and winter months in the Northern Hemisphere when flu season ramps up. By doing an Internet provider lookup, you could potentially map the flow of flulike symptoms throughout a country, finding hot spots and patterns. It might even be possible to predict the size and location or other dynamics of the next outbreak.

There is some precedent for this approach to flu tracking. Gunther Eysenbach used AdSense during the 2004–2005 flu season in Canada. He created an ad that would appear when a person searched for "flu" or "flu symptoms." The ad contained the text, "Do you have the flu? Fever, chest discomfort, weakness, aches, headache, cough," which linked to a generic patient education website. He found that the method "proved to be more timely, more accurate—with a total cost of Can$365.64 for the entire flu season—considerably cheaper than the traditional method of reports on influenza-like illnesses observed in clinics by sentinel physicians."[18]

In addition to tracking flu across a country (part V of this book looks at global disease trackers such as Google's Flu Trends), the AdSense approach might be used for political analysis or other areas in which people's opinions are polled. During the 2012 elections, an ad that appeared when the key word phrase "I hope Obama wins" was typed in and another one for when "I hope Obama loses" was typed in could have served as a proxy for each sentiment.

Facebook's ad system differs from Google's in that, at the time of this writing, an advertiser has access only to certain fields from a Facebook user's profile. According to the agreement terms of Facebook Ads, a person can target specific information on a person's profile, including location (city, state, province, or country), demographics (age range, gender, language, relationship status), likes and interests, and education and work.[19] At this time, advertisers don't have access to words and phrases from a person's status updates or comments. In addition, they don't have information from pictures, such as location and activity or content. (It should be noted that the terms are constantly subject to change. Facebook's emphasis on photo sharing in its mobile applications indicates an interest in having access to photographs taken on mobile devices, accompanied by rich metadata.)

Still, even with the limitations of Facebook Ads, it might be possible to effectively poll certain sentiments of people in various demographics. During the 2012 elections, for example, you could have set up an ad to appear on the pages of college-educated Facebook users who "liked" Mitt Romney or mentioned his name as an interest.

So far the idea of mining anonymous online ad metrics for near real-time sentiment hasn't been explored extensively in academia. But it's an approach that could prove effective, timely, and inexpensive for individuals looking to gain access to popular sentiment or other factors hidden behind Google and Facebook's proprietary data.

IV Tweets of Crisis

Whereas it takes a rather roundabout method to mine the Facebook and Google data mountains, Twitter's open ecosystem allows for a more straightforward approach: collect the tweets and filter and analyze the text for indicators of stress, crisis, or other sentiments. In October 2011, Global Pulse, an initiative of the United Nations Executive Office of the Secretary-General, published results from a study that examined tweets from Indonesia and the United States. The goal was to better understand the sentiment of the citizens and to add value to existing policy analysis.

The project classified tweets into categories to perform quantitative analysis of citizens' concerns. Key metrics the researchers tracked included anomalous spikes or drops in tweets about a particular topic such as power outages, weekly and monthly trends in the topics of Twitter conversations, patterns in volume of particular topics over time, proportions of different subtopics such as informal versus formal loans, and the way Twitter conversations compared to outside data sets.[20]

Global Pulse partnered with Crimson Hexagon, a company that collects and analyzes publicly available social media data. According to the company, Indonesia ranks fourth in the world for Twitter use; its citizens post 5.5 million location-tagged tweets per day. For the Global Pulse project, Crimson Hexagon had access to all publicly available tweets from July 2010 to October 2011. Using a sentiment analysis algorithm originally developed in Harvard's Quantitative Social Science Department that mines text for key words and relationships between those words, researchers were able to get a sense of the type and relative intensity of stressors about topics such as debt and the price and availability of food and fuel in Indonesia during this time.[21] Some of the topics in Indonesia were compared to Twitter conversations in the United States to see how conversations differed.

One of the findings indicates that tweets about fuel differ between the two countries. In particular, fuel tweets in the United States centered around price, whereas fuel tweets in Indonesia centered around the availability of different types, such as gasoline, diesel, oil, and kerosene. This difference suggests that further analysis should differentiate subtopics of the conversation around fuel. In addition, the researchers found that the volume of tweets about the price of rice in Indonesia tracked closely with inflation statistics.[22]

The researchers concluded that the data and text analysis could not provide a gauge for people's long-term goals and concerns. However, they found Twitter data, as an overall method of sifting for sentiment, to be extremely useful, especially when it comes to the immediate concerns of a nation's citizens.

V   Mining for Financial Futures

Although arguably the most challenging data set for a researcher or entrepreneur to get a hold of, large databases of anonymous financial data can provide a wealth of information about the state of the economy and possibly even help predict future economic crises. Big banks, of course, have access to these data and use this information to determine customer turnover, whom to loan money or provide credit to, and the interest rates that apply.

But if this sort of data were more broadly available to researchers or entrepreneurs outside the big banks, it could be a boon to behavioral economics at all scales. To get an idea of the possibilities, consider the work by Katherine Krumme at MIT (also discussed in chapter 7). In 2008, Krumme was given access to an anonymized Bank of America database of 80 million customers' financial data. A majority of the analysis was on buying patterns across demographics. Krumme found that the most predictable people most frequently spend at grocery stores and restaurants, whereas the least predictable people spend at gas stations and fast-food chains. She also found that the wealthy tend to shop at many stores during a single excursion, whereas those with fewer means tend to visit a single store at a time.[23]

This sort of analysis is just the tip of the iceberg. Coupling bank data with other sorts of data—geographic and census—one could piece together a picture of a country's economy on an unprecedented scale. One might be able to find predictors of job growth and decline or spending patterns linked to consumer confidence indexes, for instance. The latter could provide a new, up-to-the-minute consumer confidence index. The data could be used to predict the industries that will be most effected by recessions and possibly predict the extent to which they will suffer. Big-Data-driven indicators could help businesses and governments make decisions that might mitigate impending economic crises.

The personal finance start-up Mint is a good example of a company with access to millions if not billions of up-to-date financial transactions. Mint, founded in 2006, provides an easy-to-use interface for consumers to view all their financial account information either on the phone via an app or on a computer via the Web. In addition to providing its customers with basic information about their finances, Mint gives financial advice—for example, suggesting credit cards or savings accounts that might better suit a customer's needs. When Intuit, maker of the long popular personal finance software Quicken, bought Mint in 2009, it also bought all of Mint's customer data.

Currently, Mint's main focus is to provide its customers with information about their spending and saving and to infer future habits so as to present customers with the best deals on credit cards, health insurance, travel, and so on. In 2010, Mint launched MintData, a visualization tool that allowed anyone to look at the anonymous, aggregate spending of all Mint users. A person could, for instance, find the average amount spent at restaurants in Oklahoma versus the amount spent in Washington.[24] MintData has since been discontinued, but, as of this writing (2013), the company has tentative plans to launch a similar visualization tool.

If anonymized financial data from Mint's millions of customers were to become publicly available, then more people than just the handful of Intuit researchers and economists who have partnered with the company could put them under a microscope. Uncovering emerging trends in financial data could help anticipate economic disasters and help to develop data-based guides to improve depressed economies. The pairing of financial data and other data sets could even lead to predictions of flu epidemics by answering simple questions such as in which region consumers are buying more orange juice to stave off symptoms. These are still the early days of financial data analysis, but the possibilities of accessing this sort of data are compelling.

VI Conclusion

There are a number of ways to use data sets at the national scale, many of which carry with them important policy implications. Data visualizations offer a persuasive way to tell the story of the people who generate the data. When trends in data are easy to understand, either through maps, charts, animations, or interactive data explorers, policymakers are less likely to overlook regions in crisis. The goal for visualizations like these and other forms of information analysis is always to get the most up-to-date data possible, and this is where CDRs play an important role. In addition to providing an information-dense look at a population's mobility, CDRs can provide near real-time information to help address natural disasters or other crises as smartly and as quickly as possible.

To get a sense for the feelings of a nation, you can turn to a handful of options available via the Web giants of our age. You can mine Google and Facebook by tapping into their ad networks, creating ad campaigns, and then analyzing the resulting metrics. Twitter, with its fire hose of publicly available data, is also a rich source of a population's sentiment. Using algorithms that can parse text, it's possible to extract multiple meanings in the tens of millions of 140-character missives produced daily. The trick with all of these approaches, however, is to make sure you're asking the right questions and verifying the answers you find. Chapter 9 addresses one important double-checking mechanism: putting the individual back into the loop at the global scale.

V   Reality Mining the World's Data (100 Million to 7 Billion People)

9 Gathering the World's Data: Global Census, International Travel and Commerce, and Planetary-Scale Communication

One of the most profound applications of Reality Mining is tracking and predicting disease and epidemics. In our globally connected world, deadly diseases can spread at catastrophic speed to unprecedented numbers of people. This last part explores data at the global scale, with an eye toward the goal of better understanding how diseases propagate throughout our massively connected world. Thanks to data sets that tell us how people move, what they search for online, and how they feel, we have the opportunity to create an information-based concept of how the world works.

Just as nations of the world coordinate population surveys, the World Bank, the United Nations, and other international organizations have launched and maintained efforts to collect data transnationally. Motivated by the Millennium Development Goals (MDG), a set of eight goals for 2015 ranging from halving extreme poverty to halting the spread of HIV/AIDS,[1] these international organizations have established plans and guidelines to standardize and coordinate data collection within and across countries and have launched international data-collection initiatives.

Of course, as discussed with respect to national census data in part IV, global census data are static. Thus, to quantify the movement of a population, a step crucial in modeling the spread of disease, we must also look at data sets of networks such as airline travel and shipping routes. Billions of people ride planes each year, each person with the potential to introduce a disease to a new population. And although sea shipments don't carry nearly as many people as planes, shipments of food and goods can inadvertently harbor invasive species that could carry problematic viruses, bacteria, or parasites.

At the global scale, one of the most compelling sources of data is Internet search queries, offering a window into human behavior and environmental conditions. Google's database of anonymous search terms, identified by Internet provider address but not by a specific individual if one is not signed in to a Google account, is one of the most powerful data sets available at this scale (a complicated fact and one of concern if governments access data unlawfully). Google itself makes some of its data publicly available in such useful tools as Google Flu Tracker and Insight for Search. Both of these tools demonstrate that anyone can visualize search term popularity over time and download useful data to do further analysis.

Twitter, too, can be tapped at the global scale. In this chapter, we discuss the various methods of accessing some of the Twitter fire hose, which generates hundreds of millions of tweets every day.

With such global data, it can be easy to jump to hasty conclusions about the reality on the ground. Models developed from data at large scales should be corroborated as often as possible with the experience of individuals to provide a top-down view with a bottom-up reality check. To this end, international start-up Jana developed a mobile phone mechanism to gather on-the-ground insight. The company offers the opportunity for mobile subscribers to earn small amounts of airtime in more than 100 countries throughout the world. One common way for people to earn airtime on their mobiles is by completing a survey that can involve a wide range of topics—simple questions such as whether a certain product is on the shelves at a local shop or if the respondent has recently experienced the onset of flulike symptoms. Self-report survey data provide an important, nonintrusive method of gathering real-time data that can validate the assumptions of the analysis made from the population-level data.

This chapter takes a look at the various ways in which global-scale data are collected, with an eye toward one of the most compelling applications of Big Data: tracking, predicting, and eradicating disease pandemics.

I Coordinating a Global Census

International organizations such as the World Bank, the United Nations Statistical Commission,[2] the Organization for Economic Co-operation and Development, and the International Monetary Fund have incentives to ensure that the data collected about participating countries meet a certain standard. As such, they work together to develop appropriate frameworks and best-practice policies for statistics, agreeing on indicators to track and establishing data-exchange processes and methods. The World Bank compiles international data sets based on data from national statistics systems, bound by these best practices. In addition, it also supports programs to collect data globally, such as the Marrakech Action Plan for Statistics (MAPS) and the Partnership in Statistics for Development in the 21st Century (PARIS21).[3]

MAPS[4] is a set of six actions aimed at improving international and national statistics systems. Motivated by the MDG, it includes the following three actions specific to data collection on the global scale: planning statistical systems and preparing national statistical development strategies for all low-income countries by 2006; ensuring full participation of developing countries in the 2010 census round; and setting up the International Household Survey Network, a global collection of household-based socioeconomic data sets.[5]

PARIS21[6] is an international collaboration between policymakers and analysts. Established in 1999, this forum promotes, influences, and helps countries use statistics in the most effective and meaningful ways. It assists "low-income and lower middle-income countries design, implement and monitor National Strategy for the Development of Statistics"—essentially an approach to establish uniform data collection—"and to have nationally owned and produced data for all MDG indicators."[7]

Thanks to the coordinated efforts by worldwide organizations, transnational data and global census data are now available with the reasonable expectation of consistency and standards. Data sets available online through the World Bank,[8] the Organization for Economic Cooperation and Development,[9] and the International Monetary Fund[10] in particular provide a powerful snapshot of an entire global community.

II   Trails of People and Goods

Perhaps nothing is a better proxy for human mobility at the global scale than national and international airline routes. In 2011 in the United States, there were 730 million passengers on commercial aircraft.[11] That same year airplanes shuttled 2.8

billion passengers globally.[12] The routes people take to get from A to B can be cross-correlated with census data, maps of disease, and other data sets to provide insight into the spread of information, trade, and disease.

One major source of these routes is the International Air Transport Association (IATA), which has maintained a database of information collected from domestic and international airlines since 2000. The database represents about 90 percent of global scheduled traffic recorded on a monthly basis from more than 130 carriers. It is downloadable from the IATA site,[13] and a twelve-month subscription can be purchased for about $1,000.[14] A 2006 *Proceedings of the National Academy of Sciences* paper by Vittoria Colizza and her colleagues used the IATA data of airport pairs connected by direct flights and the number of available seats on any given connection for the year 2002.[15] The resulting network contained 3,880 vertices (airports) and 18,810 edges (passenger flow between airports), which the researchers used to inform a model of the spread of global disease.

Another source of air-passenger data comes from UBM Aviation, which sells data, analytics, and consulting services on global aviation.[16] As of July 2012, UBM Aviation's data-compilation company OAG databases included more than 900 airlines and more than 4,000 airports.[17] The company also offers historic schedules of flight information dating back to 1979.[18] OAG logs reports from airlines about the number of seats on the plane and the cities of origin and destination for the flights.[19] A number of researchers have used OAG databases to estimate disease spread.[20] These databases can be purchased through the OAG website with prices varying by country, type of data, and subscription model; the OAG Flight Guide Worldwide costs $845 for a year's subscription in the United States, for instance.

In addition to airlines, cargo ships offer some insight into human mobility. Although more goods than people move about by sea (composing 90 percent of the world's trade), shipping networks can still play a major role in the spread of invasive species and diseases.

In 2001, ships and ports began to install Automatic Identification System (AIS) equipment, thereby automatically digitizing the comings and goings of sea traffic. Although AIS is used mainly to avoid collisions and increase port security, the system has had the auxiliary benefit of producing a vast database of shipping networks. Pablo Kaluza and his colleagues accessed historic AIS data for 2007 via the Sea-web database,[21] an online log of maritime statistics, including arrivals and departures of ships, to which subscriptions are available at varying costs (depending on the metric and number of users), from $630 to $14,000.[22] Using the data, Kaluza and his colleagues tracked more than 16,000 ships and nearly 1,000 ports, linking more than 36,351 pairs of arrival and departure ports. Based on itineraries of major cargo ships during 2007, the researchers found that three distinct travel modes emerged between bulk dry carriers, container ships, and oil tankers. For instance, container ships follow regularly repeating routes, whereas bulk dry carriers and oil tankers move less predictably between ports.[23]

III   Searching Web Searches

According to Statistic Brain, which compiled Google official history and Comscore data, search giant Google fields an average of 4.7 billion web queries a day, with 1.7 trillion searches in 2011 alone.[24] Within these searches are clues to people's interests and conditions. The company has even correlated flu outbreaks to the frequency of search terms (see further explanation in chapter 10). Likewise, many other trends can be uncovered by investigating the popularity, frequency, and cyclic nature of searches.

Google offers a free public tool called Trends that allows anyone to search web searches, looking for changes over time.[25] It uses data from billions of anonymous user search queries and can be downloaded as long as a user is logged into his or her Google Account.[26]

IV   Global Data from the Social Networks

Discussion of global-scale data online isn't complete without mentioning Twitter and Facebook. As mentioned in chapters 7 and 8, Twitter has a "fire hose API" that enables researchers and entrepreneurs to access a substantial fraction of all tweets. Numerous books have been written on the topic of making sense of Twitter data. Here, we provide a handful of data source options that can be useful for customizable analysis.

By mid-2012, Twitter claimed to generate more than 400 million tweets a day[27] from more than 140 million users worldwide.[28] In August 2012, Twitter announced its certified partner program, highlighting 12 partners such as DataSift, Gnip, Topsy, and others.[29] Each company has a different goal and approach, but all have deep access to Twitter's data and data insight. These companies, in turn, parse data in a number of ways and then offer presorted data sets and services to other companies and individuals interested in various insights via Twitter. Want to find tweets and conversations about the 2012 presidential election? DataSift uses natural-language processing and other filters to collect and collate these tweets. And it offers products that range in price from \$3,000 to \$15,000 a month,[30] depending on units of data received and services offered.

For those who prefer to plug into Twitter themselves, there are options for Reality Mining via its own APIs, which are, according to the company, constantly evolving.[31] One applicable API is for search, designed to query Twitter for content such as key words, tweets referencing a specific user, or tweets from a specific user. This API has limitations, however. It is not a complete index of tweets: it cannot search tweets older than a week, and search terms are limited in complexity.[32] Twitter's streaming API[33] does better than the search API, allowing larger numbers of key words to be tracked and geotagged tweets from a certain region to be collected, for instance. A fraction of all tweets from a random sampling, up to a rate limit, is pushed through this API.[34]

As discussed in chapter 7, one way of accessing Facebook's data is through advertising analytics, but another way is by tapping the company's Open Graph tool for developers. In 2010, the company offered the Open Graph protocol, which provides access to the publicly available parts of a person's social graph, including friends, photos, events, and pages. Each object in the social graph has a unique ID and can be called by that ID via the graph API.[35] The standard version of the graph API allows a person to retrieve only one piece of information per request. Batching[36] allows a person up to 50 requests at a time. By serial batching, a programmer who has written a popular application for the social-networking site can quickly tap into millions of Facebook users, but only if those users authorize the application access to their data.

Both Facebook and Twitter are evolving companies that alter access to certain amounts or types of data in certain ways. Both companies have given and continue to give to researchers novel insights into the way people on a global scale think, move, and behave, and they are therefore important stores of data for Reality Mining.

V Reality-Mining Reality Checks

The top-down, God's-eye view of the world via mass amounts of data can provide unprecedented access to emerging trends in various corners of the world. But if there's no mechanism to double-check the conclusions derived from the petabytes of global data, the models created from those data might not be as valuable as people hope. In addition to providing insight into people's mobility at this scale through CDRs (see part IV), mobile phones can serve as a useful check on an individual's state and environment.

In an early example of the importance of these reality checks comes a study of cholera outbreaks in Rwanda. Nathan Eagle worked with the public-health community and local telecommunication companies in Rwanda in 2009 to determine if people's mobility, as determined by CDRs, could predict outbreaks. The main indicator of an impending outbreak, the researchers believed, was decreased mobility within infected communities. They suspected that decreased mobility was a result of flulike symptoms, and at first it seemed to predict a cholera outbreak a week in advance.

However, the reduction in movement within these communities turned out not to be due to the population's suffering from the onset of flulike symptoms, but to heavy rains that washed out the roads. The model detected this reduction in movement from the flooding rather than from cholera. Although the detected flooding was a precursor to the cholera outbreaks, the reduction in movement turned out not to have anything to do with the onset of flulike symptoms. But with only a global view, the connection between low mobility and illness stood out rather than the actual infrastructure problem.

Thanks to unique relationships between Eagle and mobile carriers around the world, he was able to launch Jana (formerly txteagle) in 2009, a company that allows global brands to easily connect with people via mobile phones. By mid-2013, Jana reached 3.5 billion people worldwide. One of Jana's major goals is to collect consumer insights in emerging markets, where traditional market research isn't always effective or efficient. Jana offers incentives for people to opt in to research panels. Jana users provide their opinions and insights in return for extra airtime on their phone. The company is building a self-service interface to enable researchers to send custom surveys to mobile phone subscribers in more than 100 countries. In this way, Jana provides a method of gaining insight directly from a sample of 3.5 billion mobile subscribers, providing the entry point for worldwide reality checks for Big-Data analytics.

VI Conclusion

For the first time in history, humanity has the ability to view its behavior on a global scale. Various censuses, networks of travel and shipping, Web-based search, social network behavior, and mobile phone usage are playing crucial roles in this ability. Part of the reason for this development is the increased physical and digital connectivity between people, which has also led to an increased speed and scope in the spread of diseases. The next chapter explores in depth the possible applications surrounding the issue of epidemic tracking, modeling, and predicting.

10   Engineering a Safer and Healthier World

Today's world has become wrapped in data, from flight networks to call data records and Web searches to Facebook status updates. At the global scale, there may be no more worthy application of Big Data than developing a systematic way to improve health worldwide. This final chapter focuses solely on approaches for using global data to identify and stop the spread of infectious diseases, ranging from influenza to malaria. We look at the ways data described in the previous chapter can inform models of particular disease spread worldwide.

Disease travels via people, insects, and other vectors. In order to understand how disease spreads, quantifying vector movement is crucial. One way to gather mobility information is to use data on airline and shipping routes. This gross measure of movement, introduced in the previous chapter, has proven to be an important way to improve existing models of disease transmission. This chapter looks at the ways travel and shipping data can provide a more accurate view of some specific global disease vectors such as severe acute respiratory syndrome.

Models can be improved further by incorporating not only the movement of planes and boats, but also by including the discrete paths taken by individuals. With more than 6.5 billion active mobile phone subscriptions around the world, CDRs have the potential to add tremendous value to traditional epidemiological models. In addition, when CDRs are coupled with data from just-in-time mobile surveys asking subscribers about their immediate health conditions, mobile phones can become a powerful early-warning system for epidemics.

General mobility and communication behavior can be a good indicator of a person's state of mind and health, but search terms provide extra insight: they indicate explicit interest in a topic. As discussed in the previous chapter, Google's corpus of global search terms can be leveraged to provide a qualitative comparison between terms over time, as tools such as Google Trends demonstrate. But when targeted to specific applications, such as monitoring people's interest in the flu, search terms can become a uniquely powerful database for public health. Google Flu Tracker is an excellent example of how making use of pre-existing Big Data, cleverly parsing and matching it to existing databases of flu trends, can lead to a tool that allows anyone to see flu epidemic propagation in near real time. The researchers at Google have taken this concept and extended it to dengue fever, illustrating the possibility of useful applications beyond seasonal flu tracking.

Similar to Google, Facebook and Twitter harbor huge amounts of data about people's intentions, opinions, and current conditions. Within recent years, Twitter in particular has emerged as a target for public-health researchers. Researchers mine the health sentiments expressed in tweets and develop natural-language processing algorithms to disambiguate between tweets (for example, describing an individual's personal symptoms versus more widespread news on an epidemic). Much of this early-stage research focuses mostly on flu tracking because preexisting databases can be used to validate it. But some researchers are branching out to retrieve individual symptom descriptions of more general health conditions such as allergies, obesity, and bodily aches and pains.

This chapter highlights the potential impact global data can have on public health by identifying and, we hope, squelching epidemics before they can wreak havoc.

I In the Sky and on the Sea

Countries have long kept track of who catches which diseases. National databases keep records going back decades. In England and Wales, for instance, data on measles epidemics are available in two-week segments from 1948 to the present.[1] These historic databases have appealed to mathematicians and epidemiologists because they can be used to create mathematical models that represent the spread of the disease. The database can be used to identify the disease's origin and quantify its movement. Mathematicians compare these historic patterns to preexisting models that can describe any sort of propagation throughout a system. By adjusting parameters in these models, they attempt to find a model that replicates the data. The thinking goes that this best-match model can then be used to predict the spread of future outbreaks.

These models generally include a parameter that describes the movement of people, one of the main factors that determine the manner in which infectious diseases spread. Human mobility has been estimated historically by making assumptions about the way people move—that is, randomly—and by using fairly crude surveys that ask small samples of hundreds or thousands of people how they have moved in the past week, month, or year. But such surveys have the innate drawbacks of inaccuracy (relying on people's faulty memory), sparseness (only a small subset of a population is surveyed at a time), and limited timeliness (traditional surveys are not operated continually).

In the early 2000s, however, epidemiologists and mathematicians realized that they could tap into data sets that offer a better sort of proxy for human movement across countries and regions. Air travel and shipping routes, both discussed in the previous chapter, can provide an indicator of the way people and goods (both capable of harboring disease vectors) move about the world.[2]

Airlines provide a built-in network that shows the manner in which cities are connected. Using data for the number of people that travel to and from airports, epidemiologists can add a layer of information to a global model of disease spread that's not possible when simply assuming the mobility of people from sparse data sets.

In 2006, Vittoria Colizza and her colleagues illustrated that the air-transportation networks are responsible for a global pattern of emerging diseases such as severe acute respiratory syndrome. The researchers even offered a model based on airline networks that they claim can provide a forecast of emergent disease outbreaks, although they concede that the use of additional factors—seasonal variation and differences between hygiene conditions and sanitation of regions, for instance—would improve the model's accuracy.[3]

But not all travel and shipping routes are of equal importance in global disease spread. In fact, only a relatively small number of air-traffic routes between cities may be needed to describe movement of an epidemic. Georgiy Bobashev, Robert J. Morris, and D. Michael Goedecke suggest that between 200 and 300 of

3,000 cities sampled can capture enough information about the spread of a disease such as influenza.[4]

Some global diseases, such as those borne of mosquitos or other pests, are better modeled by including global shipping routes as a measure of mobility in addition to passenger airline routes because insects can easily hitch a ride unnoticed on goods moved by massive cargo ships. Malaria, for example, is spread by a variety of different mosquito species. The jump of one potent species, *Anopheles gambiae*, from Africa to Brazil in the 1930s is a prime example of the way that shipping routes can play a major role in the spread of this disease. In recent years, shipping containers have introduced the Asian tiger mosquito, *Aedes albopictus*—an important vector of dengue, yellow, and West Nile fever viruses—to new areas.[5] A better understanding of the global mobility of mosquitos or other vectors transported by sea might help port cities take precautions to prevent the spread of pest-borne disease.

II   Mobile Phones and Disease Prediction

Although air and sea data can improve models, one of the most powerful ways to fine-tune those models is to look at the movement of people themselves, not just proxies. Fine-grained information about how people move can be collected via CDRs (as discussed in chapter 7). Mobility data from CDRs can be fed back into epidemiological models to help get a more accurate view of mobility as it varies from region to region within a single global model.

According to GSMA Wireless Intelligence, by the end of 2012 there will be 3.2 billion people worldwide with at least one mobile phone subscription and 4 billion by 2017.[6] (These numbers, however, are still far less than the total number of active mobile subscriptions—some people have more than one—totaling approximately 6 billion by the end of 2012.) These subscribers generate petabytes of data, effectively leaving behind a digital trail of location and communication in every country on earth. And the data are available in near real time.

Historic CDRs provide empirical, fine-grained insight into how people have moved, which can improve models, much as air and sea travel has done. CDRs contain seasonal variation in movement as well as differences in movement over regions. Although most epidemiology models assume much more static and coarse-grained conditions, models that incorporate CDRs can be more adaptive over variations in time and region.

But, importantly, the CDR data themselves can be used as a new sort of indicator for disease outbreaks, one that can be leveraged in real time. As a proof of concept, Marc Lipsitch and his colleagues deployed a mobile platform to 1 million subscribers in Mexico during the 2010 swine flu (H1N1) outbreak.[7] The platform, similar to that of Jana, as described in chapter 9, allowed users to answer surveys about their immediate health condition in exchange for one peso of airtime. Responses from surveys and passive data collected by CDRs, when combined, illustrate the possibility of correlating changes in mobile subscriber movement and communication patterns with the onset of illness.

Traditional regional warning systems for flu, for instance, have a minimal delay of days and sometimes weeks. People with symptoms don't immediately visit doctors, and local governments and hospitals don't immediately update databases with diagnosed cases. An automated tool that can tap into real-time CDRs and mobile surveys could revolutionize infectious disease surveillance in both developed and developing countries.

The cost would be low. Instead of upgrading, revamping, or expanding current disease-reporting systems, epidemiologists and governments could turn to the preexisting infrastructure of mobile phones and the data it collects for a true early-warning system. They could also tap into other data sources, such as orange juice sales or video surveillance of travelers coughing at train stations. Called "syndromic surveillance," this burgeoning field makes use of a number of scattered, different data sources to find clustered symptoms of illness in its early stages. Policymakers with systems that make use of such data could recommend early action—such as shutting down schools and universities—in time to stave off serious damage inflicted by a disease.[8]

III   Searching for Flu and Dengue

In 2009, a paper in *Nature* broke open the secrets of Big Data in a big way. The paper, written by researchers at Google, showed how web searches from millions of people could be used to estimate the level of influenza activity in various regions of the United States within a day.[9] It illustrated that Google's search query database could have applications well beyond serving up popular webpages or a relevant ad. Google effectively found a way to harness its users' interests to infer their physical condition, which it has used to design the resultant free tool Google Flu Trends.[10]

Google Flu Trends was developed from hundreds of billions of US searches: five years of anonymized Google web search logs from 2003 to 2008. But in order to find the search terms that track most closely with flu cycles, the researchers turned to public data from the US Centers for Disease Control's (CDC) Influenza Sentinel Provider Surveillance Network. They built a model of flu activity based on the CDC's public data and then compared their search query database of 50 million of the most common search terms on all topics without prefiltering. The comparison between the CDC model and the search query database revealed that, in terms of frequency and timing, certain search queries peaked in accordance with increases in flu activity according to CDC data. From this comparison, the researchers collected the 45 search queries that fit the CDC's model of yearly flu activity. Search queries fell under broad categories such as influenza complication, cold/flu remedy, general influenza symptoms, and various terms for influenza.

The method used here for validating search terms that correlate with flu activity has been repeated for at least 28 countries as well as for all 50 US states. Empirical databases[11] of flu activity for various countries are available through Google.org. In addition, Flu Trend data can be viewed as a graph of activity versus time and downloaded as a text file.

In a tool called Dengue Tracker, Google has extended its methodology for determining flu activity to determining dengue fever activity in at least 10 countries, including Bolivia, Brazil, India, Indonesia, and Singapore.[12] A 2011 paper outlines the approach researchers used to develop it, noting that this tool could be especially useful because dengue tends to strike in countries where there is a lack of resources for traditional disease surveillance.[13]

But the algorithmic approach is not perfect, and as with other Big-Data models, those based on search terms alone need verification. Google predicted in January 2013 that 11 percent of the population was suffering from flu at the season's peak, but this estimate was almost double that of the CDC at 6 percent. Some researchers suspect that the discrepancy could be explained by widespread media coverage of the flu season, with a boost from social media, but it's unclear exactly which factors caused the discrepancy.[14] This points to the importance of models that incorporate at the very least a certain amount of search context, but ideally some on-the-ground reality checks, as discussed in the next section.

IV Social Networks for Epidemics

Twitter and Facebook are two online services that may have the most explicit and detailed compilation of information on people in the world. From jobs, location, and political affiliation to sentiment, as revealed by a status update, the amount of information about themselves that people are making publicly available is mind boggling. To date, few researchers have mined Facebook for clues about global public health. In contrast, many researchers have pounced on the relatively easy-access Twitter data in recent years. These early results promise a bright future of comprehensive and reliable public-health systems that leverage social data for global health.

In 2010, Vasileios Lampos and Nello Cristianini extended the work done by Google researchers by mining hundreds of thousands of tweets per day of the 5.5 million active Twitter users in the United Kingdom for indicators of influenza. Similar to the way Google researchers found search terms that correlated with the rate of flu in a region, Lampos and Cristianini compared existing data on influenza in the United Kingdom from June to December 2009. The researchers found that certain tweets contained indicators of flu that had a more than 95 percent correlation with data from the UK Health Protection Agency during the H1N1 outbreak in 2009.[15] The Twitter-based flu tracker is an independent verification of Google's approach and could provide an improvement on the use of search terms alone. Although both online searching and tweet posting can be influenced by hype and media discussions, people might be more likely to provide explicit context on Twitter by posting statements such as "I have the flu." These sorts of statements, if detected by automated systems, could be useful in predicting the scope of the situation on the ground, in much the same way mobile surveys discussed in chapter 9 could.

Other researchers, including Eiji Aramaki[16] and his colleagues as well as Cynthia Chew and Gunther Eysenbach,[17] also analyzed tweets using various approaches. Aramaki developed a natural-language filter to distinguish between conversation about flu and tweets that indicated a person was ill. Chew and Eysenbach focused on three tactics: monitoring terms such as *H1N1*, employing content analysis to determine the intent of the tweet (to share news or to self-diagnose, for example), and validating Twitter as a real-time tracking tool.

Other researchers are looking at Twitter as a more general source of public-health data at the global scale. Michael J. Paul and Mark Dredze[18] have developed a topic model specifically designed to find words describing symptoms and treatments with various ailments. Trained on 1.6 million tweets that contained discussions of disease and illness, the Ailment Topic Aspect Model was able to isolate conditions ranging from influenza and infections to injuries, dental problems, and general aches and pains. The researchers say their model matches the early tracking results from Google Flu Trends and other specialized Twitter models built from government health databases.

Twitter mining points to the possibility of a new way of gathering public sentiment for health clues—in a sense, eavesdropping on public conversations about health rather than asking people directly. Still, more work needs to be done to validate the sentiment on the ground, perhaps in conjunction with mobile surveys, before a social health–monitoring system is robust.

V Conclusion

As a global community, we are on the cusp of a new era of public health. For epochs, humans have been at the mercy of pestilence, but as developments in medicine progressed and scientists discovered the causes of illnesses, lives were saved and suffering alleviated. Nevertheless, in modern times although scientists have understood the origins of disease, they haven't always had a clear idea about the way it spreads throughout populations. And they certainly haven't been able to predict its path with any sort of accuracy.

Now, however, scientists finally have a glimmer of the ultimate in preventative tools—Big Data. Big Data and Reality Mining have the potential to create a sort of real-time crystal ball that informs health-care providers, public policymakers, and others about acute threats such as a novel flu virus or a sudden uptick in cholera.

Part V has highlighted a number of data sources to fashion this crystal ball, from travel networks and search engine queries to mobile surveys and live Tweets. It has also underscored a number of projects that use these data sources. As we move forward in time, it's likely that the best early-warning systems for acute epidemics will be built with a combination of large pools of data sources that have ways to refer back to the individual for a reality check (either via surveys on mobile devices or via verifiable tweets). At the same time, much more work needs to be done to understand the best way to suss out information about chronic diseases via social networking, search queries, and mobile phone data. We still need a better understanding of the way our data can be correlated to chronic diseases such as diabetes, immune system disorders, and heart disease. Just as flu data were hiding in plain sight of Google engineers for nearly a decade, it's likely signals for chronic diseases are out there somewhere. They just need to be picked out from the noise.

Conclusion

In writing this book, we decided to take an approach that focused, when possible, on the start-ups or established companies that were practicing some sort of Reality Mining. Although academic papers and dissertations are interesting, they often describe fleeting research projects that may or may not lead to far-reaching initiatives or that have one-time results that can't be verified. It's certainly true that companies can flame out, be acquired, or simply fade away, but we believe that sharing examples of Reality Mining in the marketplace is a better way to ground Big-Data applications in a practical realm.

That said, upon editing, we removed a number of the companies named in early drafts of this book because they no longer existed. And it's likely some of the companies that made the cut at the time of printing won't be around in the next three to five years. The world of Big Data is moving fast. The churn of various start-ups is a testament to its speed.

We also felt, however, that academic papers do have an important place in the Big-Data landscape. After all, the term *Reality Mining* was coined in an MIT dissertation. The papers cited in this book tend to scratch the surface of possibilities with Big Data. And the truth is this: in order to fully realize the potential of petabytes of data and their thoughtful and conscientious application to human systems, engineers need to operate at a scale and over time that simply aren't possible in academia.

And so in addition to being a guide to Big-Data mining, this book is, at its core, a call to action. For those of you who are already entrepreneurs, think of the ways you, your neighbors, and the world can benefit from Reality Mining. For those of you in government, think of the ways data can be used to make the case for better policies. For those of you in academia, look at how your projects can be applied broadly and on a longer time scale. All the while, consider privacy and the way it shifts at various scales and in various social contexts. Engineer privacy into your solutions from the beginning and be transparent about your data collection and usage.

A good place to start engineering with Reality Mining is to look at systems that fail: Chronic disease management. Neighborhood blight. Organizational redundancy. Clogged highways. Economic Recessions. Worldwide pandemics.

Next, think about the types of data that act as indicators to or can be associated with these system failures: Changes in physical activity. An uptick in graffiti. Decreased worker productivity. Slow-moving cars. A change in shopping habits. Human travel patterns. This book provides pointers to various related data sets, but it's admittedly a limited sampling. Data are everywhere. Using them is just a matter of accessing them.

Consider, too, the ramifications of collecting data at each of the various scales—individual, neighborhood and organization, city, nation, and world. What privacy concerns are relevant? What incentives for data sharing are at play? When and where might transparency be most useful? Who benefits from your approach to data ownership and why?

And finally, think about not just gleaning knowledge from your data, but about putting the data into systems to make those systems run better and smarter. How can you design a mobile phone app to help a person monitor his diabetes better? How can you help citizens participate in reclaiming a decrepit neighborhood? How can knowledge workers share information more easily? What does it take to predict traffic and send travel-time estimates or alternate routes to drivers when they need them? How might particular patterns in consumer spending predicate a national recession or help allocate government stimulus money more effectively? How can human mobility be used to curb the next major pandemic?

It is, of course, naive to believe that Big Data—our constant, collective data exhaust—will be used only to improve the world. Recent events have demonstrated the sort of abuses possible when governments have access to these data: to surveil citizens, to squelch political opposition, and to impede civil liberties. In addition, a world where companies and advertisers want to determine consumers' next moves only in order to make a bigger profit, to provide just-in-time advertisements, or to coerce consumer behavior is few people's idea of progress. We leave the in-depth exploration of these troubling ramifications of imprudent uses of Big Data to other texts.

But it's also naive to believe that unscrupulous applications of Big Data mean that its collection and use should cease all together. And that's why we have proposed another way for engineers, entrepreneurs, academics, and policymakers to approach Big-Data-based systems: using data to affect positive change, all the while considering the reality of the situation on the ground and the ethical constraints inherent in dealing with personal data.

We hope this book has provided a basic overview of the positive potential of Big Data. And we hope it has pointed you toward applications, systems, and concepts inspired by a Reality-Mining approach. The era of Big Data is upon us. Go build a better world.

Notes

Introduction

1. Andrew McAfee and Erik Brynjolfsson, "Big Data: The Management Revolution," *Harvard Business Review* 90, no. 10 (2012): 60–66.

Chapter 1

1. "GSMA Announces New Global Research that Highlights Significant Growth Opportunity for the Mobile Industry," October 8, 2012, at http://www.gsma.com/newsroom/gsma-announces-new-global-research -that-highlights-significant-growth-opportunity-for-the-mobile-industry/.

2. More information on tracking depression is available at http://www .preventivemedicine.northwestern.edu/research/mobilyze.html?t=vD1.

3. More information on tracking the symptoms of Parkinson's is available at http://www.parkinsonsvoice.org/.

4. Miko Raento, Antti Oulasvirta, Renaud Petit, and Hannu Toivonen, "ContextPhone: A Prototyping Platform for Context-Aware Mobile Applications," *Pervasive Computing, IEEE* 4, no. 2 (2005): 51–59.

5. Nathan Eagle, "Machine Perception and Learning of Complex Social Systems," PhD diss., MIT, 2005.

6. The MIT consent form, "Consent to Participate in Non-biomedical Research: Inferring Social Networks Automatically Using Wearable Sensors," is available for view at http://reality.media.mit.edu/pdfs/consent.pdf.

7. Tanzeem Choudhury, Sunny Consolvo, Beverly Harrison, Jeffrey Hightower, Anthony LaMarca, Louis LeGrand, Ali Rahimi, et al., "The Mobile Sensing Platform: An Embedded Activity Recognition System," *Pervasive Computing, IEEE* 7, no. 2 (2008): 32–41.

8. Joseph F. McCarthy, David H. Nguyen, Al Mamunur Rashid, and Suzanne Soroczak, "Proactive Displays & the Experience UbiComp Project," *ACM SIGGROUP Bulletin* 23, no. 3 (2002): 38–41.

9. Matthew Laibowitz, "Parasitic Mobility for Sensate Media," MS thesis, MIT, 2004; Amiya Bhattacharya and Sajal K. Das, "LeZi-Update: An Information-Theoretic Approach to Track Mobile Users in PCS Networks," in *Proceedings of the 5th Annual ACM/IEEE International Conference on Mobile Computing and Networking*, 1–12 (Rochester, IL: ACM, 1999); Seok J. Kim and Chae Y. Lee, "Modeling and Analysis of the Dynamic Location Registration and Paging in Microcellular Systems," *IEEE Transactions on Vehicular Technology* 45, no. 1 (1996): 82–90.

10. Nathan Eagle and Alex Sandy Pentland, "Eigenbehaviors: Identifying Structure in Routine," *Behavioral Ecology and Sociobiology* 63, no. 7 (2009): 1057–1066.

11. Hong Lu, Wei Pan, Nicholas D. Lane, Tanzeem Choudhury, and Andrew T. Campbell, "SoundSense: Scalable Sound Sensing for People-centric Applications on Mobile Phones," in *Proceedings of the 7th International Conference on Mobile Systems, Applications, and Services*, 165–178 (Kraków: ACM, 2009).

12. For more on Funf and Funf Journal, go to http://www.funf.org/about.html.

13. For example, see the MobileSpy website at http://www.mobile-spy.com/ and its list of features at http://www.mobile-spy.com/spy_features.html.

14. For more on such laws, go to http://www.flexispy.com/. The spyware vendors generally stress that the software is not for use on phones that are not owned by the software user. Applicable laws and regulations vary throughout regions, states, and countries, and anyone who uses the software should be aware of these laws. A mobile phone user should check a phone for unlawful use of spyware by a third party and be aware of precautions to take in such a scenario.

15. More information on SODA is available at http://soda.techneos .com/SODAHelpCenter/MobileInstallation.html.

16. "Vicon Signs License Agreement with Microsoft to Develop New Medical Technology," October 26, 2009, at http://www.prweb.com/ releases/2009/10/prweb3048274.htm.

17. More information on SenseCam is available at http://research .microsoft.com/en-us/um/cambridge/projects/sensecam/.

18. More information on Google Glass is available at https://plus .google.com/+projectglass/posts.

19. MyLifeBits is available at http://research.microsoft.com/en-us/ projects/mylifebits/.

20. Nat Friedman, "How to Log Your Life," July 12, 2009, at http://nat .org/blog/2009/07/how-to-log-your-life/.

21. Track Your Happiness is available at http://www.trackyourhappiness .org/.

22. The your.flowing.data system is available at http://your.flowingdata .com/.

23. DailyDiary is available at http://www.dailydiary.com.

Chapter 2

1. Yuelin Lee and Nathan Eagle, "Using Cellular Phones to Capture Social Network Dynamics in Young Adult Smoking," National Institutes of Health grant, NIH R21, no. CA152074-01.

2. Chyke A. Doubeni, George Reed, and Joseph R. DiFranza, "Early Course of Nicotine Dependence in Adolescent Smokers," *Pediatrics* 125, no. 6 (2010): 1127–1133.

3. US Department of Health and Human Services, Substance Abuse and Mental Health Services Administration (SAMHSA), Office of Applied Studies, *Results from the 2007 National Survey on Drug Use and Health: National Findings*, NSDUH Series H-34, DHHS Publication No. SMA 08-4343 (Rockville, MD: SAMHSA, 2008), at http://www.samhsa.gov/data/nsduh/2k7nsduh/2k7Results.htm.

4. David W. Wetter, Susan L. Kenford, Samuel K. Welsch, Stevens S. Smith, Rachel T. Fouladi, Michael C. Fiore, and Timothy B. Baker, "Prevalence and Predictors of Transitions in Smoking Behavior among College Students," *Health Psychology* 23, no. 2 (2004): 168.

5. Nathan Cobb, Amanda L. Graham, and David Abrams, "Social Network Structure of a Large Online Community for Smoking Cessation," *American Journal of Public Health* 100, no. 7 (2010): 1282–1289.

6. Nathan Eagle and Alex Sandy Pentland, "Eigenbehaviors: Identifying Structure in Routine," *Behavioral Ecology and Sociobiology* 63, no. 7 (2009): 1057–1066.

7. Kate Greene, "TR10: Reality Mining: Sandy Pentland Is Using Data Gathered by Cell Phones to Learn about Human Behavior," *Technology Review* March/April (2008): 54.

8. Hilary Stout, "Technologies Help Adult Children Monitor Aging Parents," *New York Times,* July 28, 2010.

9. Details on these privacy rights are available at http://www.it.ojp.gov/default.aspx?area=privacy&page=1285.

10. Kristin Voigt and Harald Schmidt, "Wellness Programs: A Threat to Fairness and Affordable Care," May–September, 2009, at http://healthcarecostmonitor.thehastingscenter.org/kristinvoigt/wellness-programs-a-threat-to-fairness-and-affordable-care/.

11. Steve Lohr, "Carrots, Sticks, and Lower Premiums," *New York Times,* March 27, 2010.

12. Kris Dunn, "Tribune Company Rescinds $100/Month Penalty for Smokers, Keeps Spousal Carve Out . . . ," May 2, 2008, at http://www.hrcapitalist.com/2008/05/tribune-company.html.

13. "Health Care Reform Offers Boost to Wellness Programs," March 24, 2010, at http://www.prlog.org/10592210-health-care-reform-offers-boost-to-wellness-programs.html.

14. "Demystifying ROI: What You Can Expect from Workplace Wellness Programs," 2012, at http://www.welcoa.org/freeresources/pdf/rongoetzel011912.pdf.

15. Quoted in Susan Fahey Desmond, "Using Wellness Programs to Reduce Healthcare Costs," August 7, 2009, at http://hrhero.com/hl/articles/2009/08/07/using-wellness-programs-to-reduce-health-care-costs/.

16. Michelle M. Mello and Meredith B. Rosenthal, "Wellness Programs and Lifestyle Discrimination—the Legal Limits," *New England Journal of Medicine* 359, no. 2 (2008): 192–199.

17. Voigt and Schmidt, "Wellness Programs."

18. Ari Allyn-Feuer, "Pay-as-You-Drive Insurance, Privacy, and Government Mandates," July 17, 2009, at http://arstechnica.com/tech-policy/2009/07/eff-to-ca-metered-auto-insurance-is-still-a-slippery-slope/.

19. Karen Eltis, "Predicating Dignity on Autonomy: The Need for Further Inquiry into the Ethics of Tagging and Tracking Dementia Patients with GPS Technology," *Elder LJ* 13 (2005): 387.

20. "California Counties See a Rise in Elder Abuse," January 26, 2013, at http://www.premierlegal.org/california-counties-see-a-rise-in-elder-abuse/.

21. "Congress Targets Senior Abuse in Elder Justice Act as Part of Health Care Reform," November 23, 2009, at http://seniorjournal.com/NEWS/Opinion/2009/20091123-CongressTargets.htm.

22. More information about "geofences" is available at http://www.geonovo.com/geofence-elderly-wanderers.html.

23. Bruce Vielmetti, "Lawsuit Accuses GPS Firm of Aiding Domestic Abuse," April 23, 2010, at http://www.jsonline.com/news/milwaukee/91985944.html.

24. Jeff Welty, "GPS Tracking for Domestic Violence Offenders?" May 11, 2009, at http://sogweb.sog.unc.edu/blogs/ncclaw/?p=345; Kimberly Rosen, "GPS Monitoring can Curb Domestic Violence," April 10, 2009, at http://www.maine.gov/legis/house_gop/opinion/rosen_gpsdviolence.htm.

25. Ariana Greene, "More States Use GPS to Track Abusers," *New York Times*, May 8, 2009.

Chapter 3

1. For more information on the ethics of and rules for using humans in projects at MIT, see the Committee on the Use of Humans as Experimental Subjects (COUHES) website at http://web.mit.edu/committees/couhes/.

2. Liam Tung, "Microsoft to Tag Conference-Goers with RFID," August 25, 2008, at http://news.cnet.com/8301-1001_3-10024811-92.html; Patrick Thibodeau, "IBM Uses RFID to Track Conference Attendees," October 17, 2007, at http://www.computerworld.com/s/article/9042779/IBM_uses_RFID_to_track_conference_attendees.

3. "Alliance Tech Acquires Leading Face-to-Face Social Networking Technology Addition of nTAG technology and Assets Create Industry's Most Advanced Event Measurement Solution," March 23, 2009, at http://www.alliancetech.com/resources/press-releases/200903/alliance-tech-acquires-leading-face-to-face-social-networking.

4. More information on OpenKM is available at http://www.openkm.com/.

5. More information on such open-source software tools is available at http://www.manageability.org/blog/stuff/knowledge-management -open-source-java.

6. Stephen Baker, "Data Mining Moves to Human Resources," *Business Week*, March 11, 2009.

7. "Electronic Ties That Bind: Software That Spots Hidden Networks," *The Economist* (United States), June 27, 2009.

8. For more on Verint Systems Inc., see http://verint.com/solutions/ index.html.

9. Danny Wyatt, Tanzeem Choudhury, Henry Kautz, and James Kitts, "Creating Dynamic Social Network Models from Sensor Data," presented at *International Sunbelt Social Network Conference* (April 2006).

10. More information on employer rights to listen to phone calls is available at http://www.privacyrights.org/fs/fs7-work.htm#2a.

11. More information about text-message privacy on an employer-provided mobile phone is available at http://www.privacyrights.org/fs/ fs7-work.htm#4e.

12. The *City of Ontario v. Quon* decision is available at http://www .supremecourt.gov/opinions/09pdf/08-1332.pdf.

13. Prabal Dutta, Paul M. Aoki, Neil Kumar, Alan Mainwaring, Chris Myers, Wesley Willett, and Allison Woodruff, "Common Sense: Participatory Urban Sensing Using a Network of Handheld Air Quality Monitors," in *Proceedings of the 7th ACM Conference on Embedded Networked Sensor Systems*, 349–350 (Rochester, IL: ACM, 2009).

14. Min Mun, Sasank Reddy, Katie Shilton, Nathan Yau, Jeff Burke, Deborah Estrin, Mark Hansen, Eric Howard, Ruth West, and Péter Boda, "PEIR, the Personal Environmental Impact Report, as a Platform for Participatory Sensing Systems Research," in *Proceedings of the 7th International Conference on Mobile Systems, Applications, and Services*, 55–68 (Rochester, IL: ACM, 2009).

15. Sasank Reddy, Katie Shilton, Gleb Denisov, Christian Cenizal, Deborah Estrin, and Mani Srivastava, "Biketastic: Sensing and Mapping for Better Biking," in *Proceedings of the 28th International Conference on Human Factors in Computing Systems*, 1817–1820 (Rochester, IL: ACM, 2010).

16. George Danezis, Stephen Lewis, and Ross Anderson, "How Much Is Location Privacy Worth?" In *Fourth Workshop on the Economics of Information Security* (Cambridge, MA: Harvard University, 2005) http://infosecon .net/workshop/pdf/location-privacy.pdf.

Chapter 4

1. Nathan Eagle and Alex Pentland, "Social Serendipity: Mobilizing Social Software," *Pervasive Computing, IEEE* 4, no. 2 (2005): 28–34.

2. More information about Blendr is available at http://blendr.com/ help/?section=21.

3. Alyson Shontell, "Foursquare's Smart Move to Block a Creepy Stalking App Makes Facebook Look Really Bad," April 1, 2012, at http://www .businessinsider.com/foursquares-smart-move-to-block-a-creepy -stalking-app-makes-facebook-look-really-bad-2012-4.

4. More information on Project Noah is available at http://www .networkedorganisms.org.

5. For the squirrel project, go to http://www.projectsquirrel.org/index .shtml.

6. For the ladybug project, go to http://www.lostladybug.org/.

7. Geoffrey Fowler, "Apps Pave Way for City Services," *Wall Street Journal*, November 18, 2010, http://online.wsj.com/news/articles/SB100014 24052748704658204575611143577864882.

8. More information on Open 311 is available at http://open311.org/ about?.

9. Paul Tough, "The Poverty Clinic," *The New Yorker*, March 21, 2011.

10. Katie Shilton and Deborah Estrin. "Participatory Sensing and New Challenges to US Privacy Policy," n.d., at http://www.ntia.doc.gov/files/ntia/comments/100402174-0175-01/attachments/Shilton%20and%20Estrin%20-%20Participatory%20sensing%20challenges%20final.pdf.

Chapter 5

1. United Nations Department of Economic and Social Affairs (DESA), *World Urbanization Prospects: The 2009 Revision. Highlights*, Report no. ESA/P/WP/215 (N.p.: DESA, Population Division, 2009), at http://esa .un.org/unpd/wup/Documents/WUP2009_Press-Release_Final_Rev1 .pdf.

2. "Traffic Problems Tied to the Economy, Study Says," February 5, 2013, at http://mobility.tamu.edu/ums/media-information/press-release/.

3. Krishna Jayaraman, "'Expand to Grow' Approach: The Solution to the Increasing in the Traffic Market [*sic*]," August 22, 2011, at http:// www.frost.com/sublib/display-market-insight-top.do?id=240608758.

4. More information about traffic content is available at http://www .ttwnetwork.com/index.php/sigalert-sample.

5. Live traffic video is available at http://trafficland.com.

6. Ali Haghani, Masoud Hamedi, Kaveh Farokhi Sadabadi, Stanley Young, and Philip Tarnoff, "Data Collection of Freeway Travel Time Ground Truth with Bluetooth Sensors," *Transportation Research Record: Journal of the Transportation Research Board* 2160, no. 1 (2010): 60–68.

7. See "The Bright Side of Sitting in Traffic: Crowdsourcing Road Congestion Data," *Google, Official Blog*, August 25, 2009, at http:// googleblog.blogspot.com/2009/08/bright-side-of-sitting-in-traffic.html.

8. M. D. Siegler, "Google Maps for Mobile Crosses 200 Million Installs; In June It Will Surpass Desktop Usage," *TechCrunch*, May 25, 2011, at http://techcrunch.com/2011/05/25/google-maps-for-mobile-stats/.

9. Leena Rao, "Google Taps Kleiner-Backed Inrix to Provide Real Time Traffic Data for Maps and Navigation Apps," *TechCrunch*, September 26,

2011, at http://techcrunch.com/2011/09/26/google-taps-kleiner-backed -inrix-to-provide-real-time-traffic-data-for-maps-and-navigation-apps/.

10. More information about APIs for mapping data is available at http:// code.google.com/apis/maps/documentation/webservices/index.html.

11. "App Waze Doubles from 10 to 20 million Users in 6 Months," July 5, 2012, at http://www.businessinsider.com/traffic-app-waze-doubles -from-10-to-20-million-users-in-6-months-2012-7.

12. "I-95 Corridor Coalition with INRIX Expands Vehicle Probe Project," October 11, 2011, at http://www.inrix.com/pressrelease .asp?ID=143.

13. "Memphis PD: Keeping Ahead of Criminals by Finding the 'Hot Spots,'" May 6, 2011, at http://www-01.ibm.com/software/success/ cssdb.nsf/cs/GREE-8F8M7J?OpenDocument&site=corp&cty=en_us.

14. US Geological Survey, *The National Map*, at http://nationalmap .gov/.

15. US census information is available at http://www.census.gov.

16. Stuart Wolpert, "Fighting Violent Gang Crime with Math," October 28, 2011, at http://newsroom.ucla.edu/portal/ucla/fighting-violent -gang-crime-with-218046.aspx.

17. Erica Goode, "Sending the Police before There's a Crime," *New York Times* August 15, 2011.

18. More information on the Urban Area Security Initiative is available at http://www.fema.gov/fy-2009-urban-areas-security-initiative-nonprofit -security-grant-program.

19. Amanda Erickson, "Why City Governments Love Crime Cameras," *The Atlantic Cities* (blog), December 14, 2011, at http://www .theatlanticcities.com/technology/2011/12/why-city-governments -love-crime-cameras/726/.

20. Aundreia Cameron, *Measuring the Effects of Video Surveillance on Crime in Los Angeles* (Los Angeles: University of Southern California School of Policy, Planning, and Development, 2008).

21. Jennifer King, Deirdre Mulligan, and Steven Raphael, *CITRIS Report: The San Francisco Community Safety Camera Program* (Berkeley: University of California Center for Information Technology Research in the Interest of Society, 2008).

22. "1,000 Cameras 'Solve One Crime,'" *BBC News*, August 24, 2009, at http://news.bbc.co.uk/2/hi/8219022.stm.

23. Nancy G. La Vigne, Samantha S. Lowry, Allison M. Dwyer, and Joshua A. Markman, *Using Public Surveillance Systems for Crime Control & Prevention* (Washington, DC: Urban Institute, Justice Policy Center, September 2011), at http://www.urban.org/uploadedpdf/412402-Using-Public-Surveillance-Systems-for-Crime-Control-and-Prevention-A-Practical-Guide.pdf.

24. Eric Jaffe, "The War on Red-Light Cameras," *The Atlantic Cities* (blog), September 22, 2011, at http://www.theatlanticcities.com/technology/2011/09/cities-question-red-light-cameras/144/.

25. Marcus Nieto, "Public Video Surveillance: Is It an Effective Crime Prevention Tool?," June 1997, at http://www.library.ca.gov/crb/97/05/crb97-005.html#4amend.

26. Yunji Kim, "Cameras Surveil UCSB Students around Campus," *The Bottom Line*, November 8, 2010, at http://thebottomline.as.ucsb.edu/2010/11/cameras-surveil-ucsb-students-around-campus.

Chapter 6

1. Jim Bak, senior public relations and marketing manager at INRIX, interviewed by Kate Greene, Nashville, TN, January 19, 2012.

2. David Murphy, "Google Maps Dumps Driving Times with Traffic Estimates," *PCMag*, July 16, 2011, at http://www.pcmag.com/article2/0,2817,2388607,00.asp.

3. Daniel C. Robbins, Edward Cutrell, Raman Sarin, and Eric Horvitz, "ZoneZoom: Map Navigation for Smartphones with Recursive View Segmentation," in *Proceedings of the Working Conference on Advanced Visual*

Interfaces, 231–234 (Rochester, IL: ACM, 2004); M. Mitchell Waldrop, "TR10: Modeling Surprise," *Technology Review*, March–April 2008, at http://www.technologyreview.com/printer_friendly_article.aspx ?id=20243.

4. More information about fast emergency response is available at http://www.i95coalition.org/i95/Projects/ProjectDatabase/tabid/120/ agentType/View/PropertyID/107/Default.aspx#INFO.

5. See chapter 9 of US Department of Transportation, Federal Highway Administration, *iFlorida Model Deployment Final Evaluation Report* (Washington, DC: US Department of Transportation, January 2009), at http:// ntl.bts.gov/lib/31000/31000/31051/14480_files/chap_9.htm.

6. Duygu Balcan, Vittoria Colizza, Bruno Gonçalves, Hao Hu, José J. Ramasco, and Alessandro Vespignani, "Multiscale Mobility Networks and the Spatial Spreading of Infectious Diseases," *Proceedings of the National Academy of Sciences* 106, no. 51 (2009): 21484–21489.

7. Franklin E. Zimring, *The City That Became Safe: New York's Lessons for Urban Crime Control* (Oxford: Oxford University Press, 2011), 143–144.

8. Erica Goode, "Sending the Police before There's a Crime," *New York Times*, August 15, 2011.

9. Jacqueline Cohen, Wilpen L. Gorr, and Andreas M. Olligschlaeger, "Leading Indicators and Spatial Interactions: A Crime-Forecasting Model for Proactive Police Deployment," *Geographical Analysis* 39, no. 1 (2006): 105–127.

10. Goode, "Sending the Police before There's a Crime."

11. Dr. GovLoop, "Project of the Week: Memphis PD—Fighting Crime with Analytics!" August 21, 2011, at http://www.govloop.com/profiles/ blogs/memphis-pd-fighting-crime-with-analytics.

Chapter 7

1. American Fact Finder is available at http://factfinder2.census.gov/ faces/nav/jsf/pages/index.xhtml.

2. The different types of surveys available through American Fact Finder can be found at http://factfinder2.census.gov/faces/nav/jsf/pages/what _we_provide.xhtml.

3. The Data.gov Interactive Platform is available at https://explore.data .gov/.

4. More information on the types of data sets accessible at data.gov and the possible APIs that can be used is available at https://explore.data .gov/catalog/raw?&page=1.

5. See World Bank, "Data: For Developers," at http://data.worldbank .org/developers.

6. The World Bank data catalog is available at http://data.worldbank .org/data-catalog.

7. More on the World Bank Data Development Group is available at http://data.worldbank.org/about/development-data-group.

8. The list of World Bank member countries is available at http://www .worldbank.org/en/about/leadership/members.

9. More information on the World Development Indicators partners is available at http://data.worldbank.org/about/wdi-partners.

10. See World Bank, "Data: Data Overview," at http://data.worldbank .org/about/data-overview.

11. See World Bank, "Data: Data Quality and Effectiveness," at http:// data.worldbank.org/about/data-overview/data-quality-and-effectiveness.

12. See World Bank, "Data: Methodologies," at http://data.worldbank .org/about/data-overview/methodologies.

13. See World Bank, "Data: For Developers."

14. See Google Public Data Explorer at http://www.google.com/ publicdata/directory#!st=DATASET&start=0.

15. Charlie Savage and James Risen, "Federal Judge Finds N.S.A. Wire-taps Were Illegal," *New York Times*, March 31, 2010.

16. Latanya Sweeney, *Uniqueness of Simple Demographics in the US Population*, LIDAP-WP4 (Pittsburgh: Carnegie Mellon University, Laboratory for International Data Privacy, 2000).

17. Amirreza Masoumzadeh and James Joshi, "Anonymizing Geo-social Network Datasets," in *Proceedings of the 4th ACM SIGSPATIAL International Workshop on Security and Privacy in GIS and LBS*, 25–32 (Rochester, IL: ACM, 2011); Hui Zang and Jean Bolot, "Anonymization of Location Data Does Not Work: A Large-Scale Measurement Study," in *Proceedings of the 17th Annual International Conference on Mobile Computing and Networking*, 145–156 (Rochester, IL: ACM, 2011).

18. Sibren Isaacman, Richard Becker, Ramón Cáceres, Margaret Martonosi, James Rowland, Alexander Varshavsky, and Walter Willinger, "Human Mobility Modeling at Metropolitan Scales," in *Proceedings of the 10th International Conference on Mobile Systems, Applications, and Services*, 239–252 (Rochester, IL: ACM, 2012).

19. More information on the data Google logs from its users is available at http://support.google.com/accounts/bin/answer.py?hl=en&answer =162743&topic=25471&ctx=topic and http://lifehacker.com/5763452/ what-data-does-chrome-send-to-google-about-me.

20. More information on Facebook ads and using them is available in its "Getting Started Guide" at https://www.facebook.com/business/ products/ads.

21. More information about Facebook APIs is available at http:// developers.facebook.com/.

22. More information on Zynga is available at http://company.zynga .com/.

23. More information on app metrics is available at http://www.appdata .com/leaderboard/apps?fanbase=0&metric_select=mau&page=1&show_na=1.

24. Katherine Krumme, "How Predictable: Patterns of Human Economic Behavior in the Wild," PhD diss., MIT, 2010.

25. Tom Groenfeldt, "Tresata Offers Big Data for Financial Firms to Act on," *Forbes*, July 10, 2012, at http://www.forbes.com/sites/tomgroenfeldt/ 2012/07/10/tresata-offers-big-data-for-financial-firms-to-act-on/.

26. More information on Mint is available at http://mint.com.

Chapter 8

1. Development Seed, "About," at http://developmentseed.org/about/.

2. The World Bank data catalog is available at http://data.worldbank.org/data-catalog.

3. See World Bank, "Data: For Developers," at http://data.worldbank.org/developers.

4. See Google, "Public Data," at http://www.google.com/publicdata/ directory.

5. See Development Seed, "Battling Hunger in the Horn of Africa," at http://developmentseed.org/projects/wfp-famine/.

6. The interactive census map is available at http://www.npr.org/censusmap/#4.00/41.83/-79.32.

7. The interactive Opportunity-Index map is available at http://opportunityindex.org/#4.00/36.52/-90.23/.

8. World Bank, "Exploring Climate and Development Links," at http://climate4development.worldbank.org/.

9. Gergely Palla, Albert-László Barabási, and Tamás Vicsek, "Quantifying Social Group Evolution," *Nature* 446, no. 7136 (2007): 664–667.

10. Marta C. Gonzalez, Cesar A. Hidalgo, and Albert-László Barabási, "Understanding Individual Human Mobility Patterns," *Nature* 453, no. 7196 (2008): 779–782.

11. Palla, Barabási, and Vicsek, "Quantifying Social Group Evolution."

12. Dirk Brockmann, Lars Hufnagel, and Theo Geisel, "The Scaling Laws of Human Travel," *Nature* 439, no. 7075 (2006): 462–465.

13. Gonzalez, Hidalgo, and Barabási, "Understanding Individual Human Mobility Patterns."

14. Chaoming Song, Zehui Qu, Nicholas Blumm, and Albert-László Barabási, "Limits of Predictability in Human Mobility," *Science* 327, no. 5968 (2010): 1018–1021.

15. Amy Wesolowski and Nathan Eagle, "Parameterizing the Dynamics of Slums," in *AAAI Symposium on Artificial Intelligence and Development*, 103–108 (Menlo Park, CA: AAAI Press, 2010).

16. Ashish Kapoor, Nathan Eagle, and Eric Horvitz, "People, Quakes, and Communications: Inferences from Call Dynamics about a Seismic Event and Its Influences on a Population," in *Proceedings of AAAI Symposium on Artificial Intelligence for Development*, 51–56 (Menlo Park, CA: AAAI Press, 2010).

17. Amy Wesolowski, Nathan Eagle, Andrew J. Tatem, David L. Smith, Abdisalan M. Noor, Robert W. Snow, and Caroline O. Buckee, "Quantifying the Impact of Human Mobility on Malaria," *Science* 338 no. 6104 (2012): 267–270, at http://realitymining.com/pdfs/ScienceMalaria12 .pdf

18. Gunther Eysenbach, "Infodemiology: Tracking Flu-Related Searches on the Web for Syndromic Surveillance," in *AMIA Annual Symposium Proceedings*, vol. 2006 (Bethesda, MD: American Medical Informatics Association, 2006), 244.

19. See Facebook Ads, "Getting Started Guide," at https://www.facebook .com/business/products/ads.

20. See United Nations Global Pulse, "Research: Twitter and Perceptions of Crisis-Related Stress," December 8, 2011, http://www.unglobalpulse .org/projects/twitter-and-perceptions-crisis-related-stress.

21. J. Roberts, "Crimson Hexagon–UN Global Pulse Indonesia Twitter Research Documentation," November 28, 2011, at http://www .unglobalpulse.org/sites/default/files/Global%20Pulse-CrimsonHex -Indonesia%20Documentation_0.pdf.

22. United Nations Global Pulse, "Research: Twitter and Perceptions of Crisis-Related Stress."

23. Katherine Krumme, "How Predictable: Patterns of Human Economic Behavior in the Wild," PhD diss., MIT, 2010.

24. "Mint Opens Up Its Data: See How Spending Is Truly Trending," October 28, 2010, at http://www.mint.com/blog/updates/mint-opens -up-its-data-see-how-spending-is-truly-trending/.

Chapter 9

1. More on the United Nations MDG is available at http://www.un.org/ millenniumgoals/bkgd.shtml.

2. The United Nations Statistics Division website is at http://unstats .un.org/unsd/default.htm.

3. See World Bank, "Data: The International System," at http://data .worldbank.org/about/data-overview/the-international-system.

4. More information on MAPS is available at World Bank, "Statistical Capacity," at http://web.worldbank.org/WBSITE/EXTERNAL/DATASTATISTICS/ SCBEXTERNAL/0,,contentMDK:20951847~menuPK:2640568~pagePK:2 29544~piPK:229605~theSitePK:239427,00.html.

5. More information on the International Household Survey Network is available at http://www.surveynetwork.org/home/about.

6. More information on PARIS21 is available at http://www.paris21.org/ about.

7. PARIS21, "National Strategies for the Development of Statistics," available at http://www.paris21.org/NSDS.

8. See World Bank, "Use Our Data," at http://data.worldbank.org/ use-our-data.

9. Statistics from the Organization for Economic Cooperation and Development are available through its Data Lab at http://www.oecd .org/statistics/.

10. See International Monetary Fund, "World Economic Outlook Databases," at http://www.imf.org/external/ns/cs.aspx?id=28.

11. "December 2011 Airline System Traffic up 0.5 Percent from December 2010," March 22, 2012, at http://www.rita.dot.gov/bts/sites/rita.dot .gov.bts/files/press_releases/2012/bts014_12/html/bts014_12.html.

12. Tony Tyler, *IATA: 2012 Annual Review* (Beijing: IATA, 2012), at http://www.iata.org/about/Documents/annual-review-2012.pdf.

13. The IATA database is available at http://www.iata.org/Pages/default .aspx.

14. More information about airline traffic statistics is available at http:// www.iata.org/publications/Pages/carrier-tracker.aspx.

15. Vittoria Colizza, Alain Barrat, Marc Barthélemy, and Alessandro Vespignani, "The Role of the Airline Transportation Network in the Prediction and Predictability of Global Epidemics," *Proceedings of the National Academy of Sciences* 103, no. 7 (2006): 2015–2020.

16. More information about UBM Aviation is available at http://www .ubmaviation.com/about-UBM-Aviation.

17. More information about OAG databases is available at http://www .oag.com/Aviation-Data.

18. Data about flights from the past are available at http://www .oagaviation.com/Solutions/Aviation-Data/OAG-Historical-Schedules.

19. Georgiy Bobashev, Robert J. Morris, and D. Michael Goedecke, "Sampling for Global Epidemic Models and the Topology of an International Airport Network," *PloS One* 3, no. 9 (2008): e3154.

20. Andrew J. Tatem, Simon I. Hay, and David J. Rogers, "Global Traffic and Disease Vector Dispersal," *Proceedings of the National Academy of Sciences* 103, no. 16 (2006): 6242–6247; Duygu Balcan, Hao Hu, Bruno Goncalves, Paolo Bajardi, Chiara Poletto, Jose Ramasco, Daniela Paolotti, et al., "Seasonal Transmission Potential and Activity Peaks of the New Influenza A (H1N1): A Monte Carlo Likelihood Analysis Based on Human Mobility," *BMC Medicine* 7, no. 1 (2009): 45.

21. Sea-web is available at http://www.sea-web.com.

22. Current Sea-web pricing is available at http://www.sea-web.com/module_pricing.html.

23. Pablo Kaluza, Andrea Kölzsch, Michael T. Gastner, and Bernd Blasius, "The Complex Network of Global Cargo Ship Movements," *Journal of the Royal Society Interface* 7, no. 48 (2010): 1093–1103.

24. See Statistic Brain, "Google Annual Search Statistics," June 18, 2013, at http://www.statisticbrain.com/google-searches/.

25. See Google, "Trends: Analyzing Data," at http://support.google.com/insights/bin/answer.py?hl=en&answer=92768&ctx=cb&src=cb&cbid=g311zypaqvy8&cbrank=4.

26. More information about exporting Google data is available at http://support.google.com/insights/bin/answer.py?hl=en&answer=87289&ctx=cb&src=cb&cbid=1a66z5un7ilgd&cbrank=2.

27. Matt McGee, "With 400 Million Tweets per Day, Twitter Spending 'Inordinate Resources' on Improving Content Discovery," June 7, 2012, at http://marketingland.com/twitter-400-million-tweets-daily-improving-content-discovery-13581.

28. Matt McGee, "Twitter's 6th Birthday: 140 Million Active Users, 340 Million Tweets a Day," March 21, 2012, at http://marketingland.com/twitter-six-years-old-8374.

29. Twitter, "Twitter Certified Products: Tools for Businesses," at http://blog.twitter.com/search?q=datasift.

30. The prices of DataSift products are available at http://datasift.com/pricing.

31. See Twitter, "Getting Started," at https://dev.twitter.com/start.

32. See Twitter, "Using the Twitter Search API," at https://dev.twitter.com/docs/using-search.

33. For more on Twitter's streaming API, see Twitter, "Getting Started."

34. More information on rate limits for the streaming API is available at https://dev.twitter.com/docs/faq#6861.

35. More information on Facebook's graph API is available at https://developers.facebook.com/docs/reference/api/.

36. Facebook, "Facebook Developers: Batch Requests," at https://developers.facebook.com/docs/reference/api/batch/.

Chapter 10

1. Steven Riley, "Large-Scale Spatial-Transmission Models of Infectious Disease," *Science* 316, no. 5829 (2007): 1298–1301.

2. Andrew J. Tatem, David J. Rogers, and Simon I. Hay, "Global Transport Networks and Infectious Disease Spread," *Advances in Parasitology* 62 (2006): 293–343; Riley, "Large-Scale Spatial-Transmission Models of Infectious Disease."

3. Vittoria Colizza, Alain Barrat, Marc Barthélemy, and Alessandro Vespignani, "The Role of the Airline Transportation Network in the Prediction and Predictability of Global Epidemics," *Proceedings of the National Academy of Sciences* 103, no. 7 (2006): 2015–2020.

4. Georgiy Bobashev, Robert J. Morris, and D. Michael Goedecke, "Sampling for Global Epidemic Models and the Topology of an International Airport Network," *PloS One* 3, no. 9 (2008): e3154.

5. Andrew J. Tatem, Simon I. Hay, and David J. Rogers. "Global Traffic and Disease Vector Dispersal," *Proceedings of the National Academy of Sciences* 103, no. 16 (2006): 6242–6247.

6. "GSMA Announces New Global Research That Highlights Significant Growth Opportunity for the Mobile Industry," October 18, 2012, at http://www.gsma.com/newsroom/gsma-announces-new-global-research-that-highlights-significant-growth-opportunity-for-the-mobile-industry/.

7. Marc Lipsitch, Martín Lajous, Justin J. O'Hagan, Ted Cohen, Joel C. Miller, Edward Goldstein, Leon Danon, et al., "Use of Cumulative Incidence of Novel Influenza A/H1N1 in Foreign Travelers to Estimate Lower Bounds on Cumulative Incidence in Mexico," *PLoS One* 4, no. 9

(2009): e6895; Martín Lajous, Leon Danon, Ruy López-Ridaura, Christina M. Astley, Joel C. Miller, Scott F. Dowell, Justin J. O'Hagan, Edward Goldstein, and Marc Lipsitch, "Mobile Messaging as Surveillance Tool during Pandemic (H1N1) 2009, Mexico," *Emerging Infectious Diseases* 16, no. 9 (2010): 1488.

8. Matt Crenson, "Germ Patrol: Like Never Before," CBS News, Associated Press, February 11, 2009, at http://www.cbsnews.com/2100 -224_162-527736.html; Kelly J. Henning, "Overview of Syndromic Surveillance: What Is Syndromic Surveillance?" *Morbidity and Mortality Weekly Report* (CDC) 53 (2004): 5–11.

9. Jeremy Ginsberg, Matthew H. Mohebbi, Rajan S. Patel, Lynnette Brammer, Mark S. Smolinski, and Larry Brilliant, "Detecting Influenza Epidemics Using Search Engine Query Data," *Nature* 457, no. 7232 (2008): 1012–1014.

10. Google Flu Trends is available at http://www.google.org/flutrends.

11. "Google Flu Trends: Frequently Asked Questions," at http://www .google.org/flutrends/about/faq.html.

12. More information on Google's Dengue Tracker is available at http:// www.google.org/denguetrends/.

13. Emily H. Chan, Vikram Sahai, Corrie Conrad, and John S. Brownstein, "Using Web Search Query Data to Monitor Dengue Epidemics: A New Model for Neglected Tropical Disease Surveillance," *PLoS* 5, no. 5 (2011): e1206.

14. Declan Butler, "When Google Got Flu Wrong," *Nature* 494, no. 7436 (2013): 155.

15. Vasileios Lampos and Nello Cristianini, "Tracking the Flu Pandemic by Monitoring the Social Web," in *2nd International Workshop on Cognitive Information Processing (CIP), 2010*, 411–416 (Elba, IT: IEEE, 2010).

16. Eiji Aramaki, Sachiko Maskawa, and Mizuki Morita, "Twitter Catches the Flu: Detecting Influenza Epidemics Using Twitter," in *Proceedings of the Conference on Empirical Methods in Natural Language*

Processing, 1568–1576 (Stroudsberg, PA: Association for Computational Linguistics, 2011).

17. Cynthia Chew and Gunther Eysenbach, "Pandemics in the Age of Twitter: Content Analysis of Tweets during the 2009 H1N1 Outbreak," *PLoS One* 5, no. 11 (2010): e14118.

18. Michael J. Paul and Mark Dredze, "You Are What You Tweet: Analyzing Twitter for Public Health," in *Fifth International AAAI Conference on Weblogs and Social Media (ICWSM 2011)*, 265–272 (Menlo Park, CA: AAAI Press, 2011).

Index

Note: Page numbers in italics indicate tables.